Programming in Python

Dr. Pooja Sharma

FIRST EDITION 2017

Copyright © BPB Publications, INDIA

ISBN : 978-93-8655-127-6

Distributors:

BPB PUBLICATIONS
20, Ansari Road, Darya
Ganj New Delhi-110002
Ph: 23254990/23254991

BPB BOOK CENTRE
376 Old Lajpat Rai
Market, Delhi-110006
Ph: 23861747

COMPUTER BOOK CENTRE
12, Shrungar Shopping Centre,
M.G.Road, Bengaluru -560001
Ph: 25587923/25584641

DECCAN AGENCIES
4-3-329, Bank Street,
Hyderabad-500195
Ph: 24756967/24756400

MICRO MEDIA
Shop No. 5, Mahendra Chambers, 150
DN Rd. Next to Capital Cinema, V.T.
(C.S.T.) Station, MUMBAI-400 001
Ph: 22078296/22078297

Published by Manish Jain for BPB Publications, 20, Ansari Road, Darya Ganj, New Delhi- 110002 and Printed him at Repro India Pvt. Ltd, Mumbai

Organization of the Book

Chapter 1 provides an Introduction to the programming in Python language with its history, origin, features, and limitations. Apart from that the installation of Python language at various platforms Windows, Linux and MAC is also discussed in this chapter.

Chapter 2 elaborates the basic constructs of the Python language such as keywords, variables, statements, comments, indentation, and brief discussion about data types.

Chapter 3 discusses about various operators available in Python along with the programming illustration of each. Expression evaluation according to precedence and associativity is also discussed in this chapter.

Chapter 4 focuses on control structures of the Python language viz. decision making statements, looping statements and control statements.

Chapter 5 gives the extensive information about the Python native data types such as number, strings, list, tuple, set, and dictionary in great detail with their various methods and programming illustrations.

Chapter 6 describes Python functions which includes both library and user defined functions. Their advantages and types of user defined functions are explained in detail along with a new lambda function of Python.

Chapter 7 explains the use of Python modules, which can be thought of an extension of Python functions.

Chapter 8 provides the information of errors and exceptions in Python. All the concepts of exception handling are discussed in detail.

Chapter 9 discusses about the file handling in Python. Various file attributes, modes, and associated methods, functions, and encoding are elaborated. Apart from that directory handling using Python is also discussed.

Chapter 10 illustrates the concept of object oriented programming structures (OOPS) in Python. The use of classes and objects is discussed in this chapter,

Chapter 11 presents one of the significant features of OOPS, i.e., inheritance in detail with the description of single, multiple, and multilevel inheritance.

Chapter 12 implements the concept of another features of OOPS, i.e., operator overloading in detail.

The Appendix-I is given which provides the list of Python Standard Modules with the description of each.

The bibliography is given at the end for reference of readers.

Acknowledgments

The author is always indebted and gratified to the almighty for making her capable of writing this book and accomplishing achievements. She conveys her heartiest thanks to the authorities of DAV University, Jalandhar for their cooperation. She is extremely grateful to her parents for their encouragement and support in every sphere of life. She is also thankful to her husband Raj Kumar for his persistent motivation and support throughout writing this book and her little daughter Angel.

The author is thankful to BPB Publications for their assistance and guidance on this book.

Dr. Pooja Sharma

About the Author

Dr. Pooja Sharma completed her Bachelor Degree in Computer Applications in 2005 with 4th position in the University and Master Degree in Computer Science in 2007 with Gold Medal for securing first position from Guru Nanak Dev University, Amritsar. She did her PhD in 2013 on Content Based Image Retrieval under the supervision of Dr. Chandan Singh from Punjabi University, Patiala. Her academic achievements include fellowship for regular PhD from UGC, New Delhi after qualifying UGC NET and JRF, several merit certificates, gold and silver medals in matric, higher secondary, undergraduate and post graduate levels. She has several research publications in peer reviewed International journals of Springer and Elsevier with significant Thomson Reuters impact factors. She is the reviewer of various International journals of Elsevier, IET (IEEE Computer Society), and Scientific Research and Essays. She has participated in various conferences and workshops. Her areas of specialization include Content Based Image Retrieval, Face Recognition, Pattern Recognition, and Digital Image Processing. She worked and selected at various eminent Universities and Colleges during last 10 years including Central University. Presently, she is appointed as Assistant Professor in the Department of Computer Applications, I.K. Gujral Punjab Technical University, Kapurthala.

Contents

CHAPTER 1

Introduction to Python Language

Highlights

- Introduction and history of Python language
- Features of Python
- Applications of Python
- Python interactive help
- Installing and executing Python
- How Python differ from other languages

We see that computers are capable of solving numerous problems of the real world. The problems can be as simple as to multiply two numbers or as cumbersome as to design and launch a space shuttle. This would be incorrect to assume that the computer can do all the tasks on its own. Any problem whose solution is not identified cannot be solved by a computer. The computer merely works on the set of instructions given to it by a programmer. If the computer does not understand the instructions then errors may occur and solution cannot be obtained. Therefore, it is keen responsibility of the programmer to devise a solution by giving correct instructions to the computer.

1.1. Programming Language

In order to solve a problem using computer, the programmer writes the instructions which are understandable by the computer. The computer understands only digital data either '0' or '1'. The most basic language is the machine language that uses binary '0' and '1', which a computer can understand and execute very fast without using any translator (compiler or interpreter). However, it is quite difficult to code a program in machine language. The high level languages such as (C, C++, Java) are very simple to understand by humans because these languages use English language like statements. However, an additional program such as a compiler or interpreter is required to convert the high level language into machine language. Therefore, high level languages are slower than machine languages.

In other words, we can say that people express themselves using a language that has many words. Computers use a simple language that consists of strings of 0s and 1s, with a 1 representing "on" and a 0 representing "off.". The programming language works as a translator between you and the computer. Rather than learning the computer's native language (called as *machine language*), one can make use of a programming language to instruct the computer in a way that is easier to learn and understand.

Every programming language has a particular structure with a specific syntax and semantics. Programming language is something like a code for writing down the instructions that a computer will follow. In fact, programmers often refer to their programs as computer code, or the process of implementing an algorithm. Alike other high level languages such as C, C++, Java, Python is also a programming language. In this book, we will learn Python programming language in detail.

1.2. History of Python Language

Python is a very powerful high-level, object oriented programming language. It was developed by Guido Van Rossum during 1985-1990 at the national research institute for mathematics and computer science in Netherlands. It is the derivative of several other languages such as ABC, Modulo-3, C, C++, Algol-68, SmallTalk and Unix Shell. ABC is a general-purpose programming language or programming environment, which had been developed in Netherlands, Amsterdam, at the CWI (Centrum Wiskunde & Informatica). The greatest achievement of ABC was to influence the design of Python.

The source code of Python language is available under GNU i.e., General Public License (GPL). The Python is a very easy to use language with simple syntax, which makes it perfect language for beginners. It is an interpreter based language. Interpreter is a program that converts high level program into low level program, i.e., machine code. It is designed to be highly readable because it uses English keywords very frequently whereas other languages use punctuations. Moreover, it has fewer syntactical constructions than other languages.

Guido Van Rossum published the first version of Python code (version 0.9.0) in February 1991. This release included already exception handling, functions, and the core data types of list, dict, str and others. Python was developed to be module as well as object oriented language. Another version 1.0 of Python was released in January 1994. The major new features included in this release were the functional programming tools lambda, map, filter and reduce, which Guido Van Rossum never liked. Six and a half years later in October 2000, Python 2.0 was introduced. This release included list comprehensions, a full garbage collector and it had the support for Unicode. Python flourished for another 8 years in the versions 2.x before the next major release as Python 3.0 (also known as "Python 3000" and "Py3K"). Python 3 is not backwards compatible with Python 2.x. The emphasis in Python 3 had been on the removal of duplicate programming constructs and modules.

1.3. Origin of Python Programming Language

At the time when he began implementing Python, Guido van Rossum was reading the published scripts from "Monty Python's Flying Circus" (a BBC comedy series from the seventies). It occurred to him that he needed a name that should be short, unique, and slightly mysterious, so he decided to call the language Python.

1.4. Features of Python

The Python language exhibits numerous features, which are detailed as under:

Beginner's Language: Python is a great language for beginner level programmers, which supports the development of a wide range of applications from simple text processing to web browsers to games.

Easy to Learn: Python has simple structure, a few keywords, and clearly defined syntax.

Easy to Read: It is clearly defined language that is a non-programmer understands it very easily.

Easy to Maintain: The source code of Python language is quite easy to maintain.

Interpreted: It is interpreter based language. The programmer does not need to compile the code before executing the program similar to PERL and PHP. Python has a built-in debugging feature.

Interactive: Python programs can be directly written to the Python prompt by which user directly interacts with the interpreter.

Object Oriented: It supports object oriented style of programming that encapsulates code within objects. OOP breaks up code into several units that pass messages back and forth using classes.

Versatile: Python modules are capable to work with multiple operating systems and user interfaces including images and sounds.

Broad Standard Library: Python language's bulk library is portable and cross platform compatible with UNIX, Windows and Macintosh.

Interactive Mode: Python language has support for interactive mode, which allows interactive testing and debugging of code.

Portable: Python language can be executed on wide variety of hardware platforms and has similar interface on all the platforms.

Databases: Python language provides the facility of interfaces to all major commercial databases.

GUI Programming: Python provides graphical user interface (GUI) applications that can be created and ported to many system calls, libraries and Windows systems such as Windows MFC, MAC, and the X Window system of Unix.

Scalable: It provides a better structure and support for large programs.

1.5. Limitations of Python

As we see, Python language has many features, it has some limitations also as under:

- Python is an interpreter based language. Therefore, it is bit slower than compiler based languages.
- Since, Python is a high level language like C/C++/Java, it also uses many layers to communicate with the operating system and the computer hardware.
- Graphics intensive applications such as games make the program to run slower.

1.6. Major Applications of Python

The list of companies that use Python include the following:

- Yahoo! (for Yahoo! Maps)
- Google (for its spider and search engine)
- Linux Weekly News (published by using a web application written in Python)

- Industrial Light & Magic (used in the production of special effects for movies such as The Phantom Menace and The Mummy Returns).

1.7. Getting Python

The most up-to-date and current source code, binaries, documentation, news, etc., is available on the official website of Python: http://www.python.org/

The complete Python documentation can be obtained from the following the site www.python.org/doc/. The documentation is available in HTML, PDF and PostScript formats.

1.8. Installing Python

Python distribution is available for a wide variety of platforms. You need to download only the binary code applicable for your platform and install Python.You need a C compiler to compile the source code manually, if the binary code for your platform is not available. The installation of Python at various platforms like Unix and Linux is given as follows

1.8.1. Unix and Linux Installation

Here are the simple steps to install Python on Unix/Linux machine.

- Open a Web browser and go to http://www.python.org/download/ as presented in Fig. 1.1.
- Follow the link to download zipped source code available for Unix/Linux.
- Download and extract files.
- Edit the *Modules/Setup* file if you want to customize some options.
- run ./configure script
- make
- make install

This will install python in a standard location */usr/local/bin* and its libraries at*/usr/local/lib/pythonXX* where XX is the version of Python that you are using.

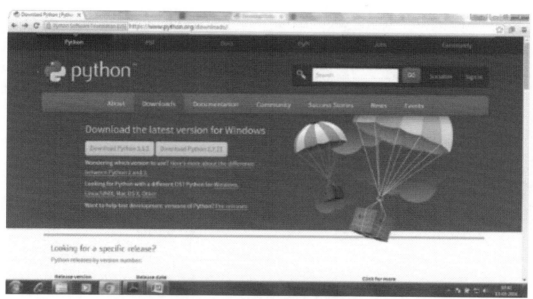

Fig. 1.1. Python Download

1.8.2. Windows Installation

Here are the steps to install Python on Windows machine.

- Open a Web browser and go to http://www.python.org/download/ as shown in the Fig 1.1.

- Follow the link for the Windows installer python-XYZ.msi file where XYZ is the version you need to install.

- To use this installer *python-XYZ.msi*, the Windows system must support Microsoft Installer 2.0. Save the installer file to your local machine and then run it to find out if your machine supports MSI.

- Run the downloaded file. This brings up the Python install wizard, which is really easy to use. Just accept the default settings, wait until the install is finished, and you are done.

1.8.3. Macintosh Installation

Recent Macs come with Python installed, but it may be several years out of date. See http://www.python.org/download/mac/ for instructions on getting the current version along with extra tools to support development on the Mac as shown in the Fig. 1.2. For older Mac OS's before Mac OS X 10.3 (released in 2003), MacPython is available."

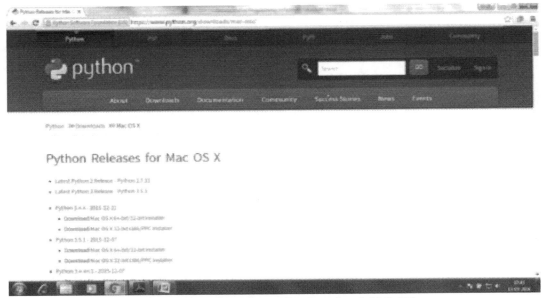

Fig. 1.2. Python Installation for MAC OS

1.9. Setting up Path

Many directories contain programs and other executable files, therefore, the operating system Windows, Unix/Linux, or MAC search for executables by providing a search path for directories. The path is a named string maintained by the operating system and is stored in an environment variable. The environment variable contains information available to the command shell and other programs.

The Unix is a case sensitive operating system. However, Windows does not follow case sensitivity. So, path variable is named as PATH in Unix or Path in Windows. On the other hand, in Mac OS, all the path details are handled by the installer.The path variable of your operating system is needed to be set before invoking the Python interpreter from any particular directory.

1.9.1. Setting up Path at Unix/Linux

Since many shells are available in Unix/Linux OS, the path set up is slightly different for different shells. For csh, bash, sh, and ksh shells the Python path can be set as follows for a particular session in Unix:

- In the csh shell: type setenv PATH "$PATH:/usr/local/bin/python" and press Enter.
- In the bash shell (Linux): type export PATH="$PATH:/usr/local/bin/python" and press Enter.
- In the sh or ksh shell: type PATH="$PATH:/usr/local/bin/python" and press Enter.

Note: /usr/local/bin/python is the path of the Python directory

1.9.2. Setting up Path at Windows

To add the Python directory to the path for a particular session in Windows:

- At the command prompt: type path %path%;C:\Python and press Enter.

Note: C:\Python is the path of the Python directory

1.10. Python Environment Variables

Here are important environment variables, which can be recognized by Python:

- PYTHONPATH: This variable plays the similar role as PATH. It is sometimes preset by the Python installer. Its task is to tell the Python interpreter where to locate the module files imported into a program. It must include the source library directory and directories containing Python source codes.

- PYTHONSTARTUP: It contains the path of an initialization file containing Python source code. It is executed every time you start the interpreter. It is named as .pythonrc.py in Unix and it comprises of commands that load utilities or modify PYTHONPATH.

- PYTHONCASEOK: It is used in Windows to instruct Python to find the first case-insensitive match in an import statement. In order to activate this variable set it to any value.

- PYTHONHOME: It is another module search path. It is usually embedded in the PYTHONSTARTUP or PYTHONPATH directories to make switching module libraries easy.

1.11. Running Python

There are three different ways to start Python:

- Interactive Interpreter
- Script from the Command Line
- Integrated Development Environment

1.11.1. Interactive Interpreter

You can start Python from DOS, Unix, or any other system that provides you a command-line interpreter or shell window. Enter python at the command line, which opens python interpreter as displayed in Fig. 1.3. It displays information about Python version, i.e, 3.5.1., the date it was released and a few options of what can be pursued next.

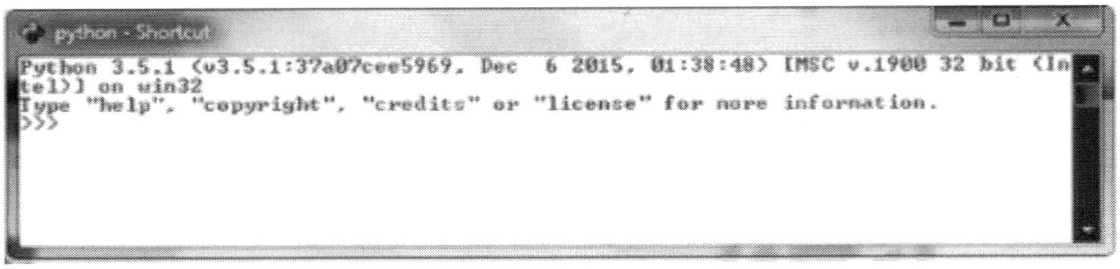

Fig. 1.3. Python interpreter version 3.5.1.

Here is the list of all the available command line options in Table 1.1.:

Option	Description
-d	provide debug output
-O	generate optimized bytecode (resulting in .pyo files)
-S	do not run import site to look for Python paths on startup

-v	verbose output (detailed trace on import statements)
-X	disable class-based built-in exceptions (just use strings); obsolete starting with version 1.6
-c cmd	run Python script sent in as cmd string
File	run Python script from given file

Table. 1.1. List of command line options

1.11.2. Script from the Command-line

A Python script can be executed at command line also. This can be done by invoking the interpreter on your application, as displayed below:

```
$python script.py  #Unix/Linux
or
python % script.py  #Unix/Linux
or
c:>python script.py  #Windows/DOS
```

1.11.3. Integrated Development Environment

Python can be run from a Graphical User Interface (GUI) environment as well, if you have a GUI application on your system that supports Python.

- **Unix:** IDLE is the very first Unix IDE for Python.
- **Windows:** PythonWin is the first Windows interface for Python.
- **Macintosh:** The Macintosh version of Python is available from the main website along with the IDLE IDE, downloadable as either MacBinary.

1.12. First Python Program

We can execute the Python program in two different modes of programming viz. interactive mode programming and script mode programming. Each of them is elaborated as follows:

1.12.1. Interactive Mode Programming

In interactive mode programming, interpreter is invoked and the programmer can code statements directly to the interpreter without passing a script file as a parameter. Open up the Python interpreter and it brings up with the following information:

```
$ python
Python2.4.3(#1,Nov112010,13:34:43)
[GCC 4.1.220080704(RedHat4.1.2-48)] on linux2
Type"help","copyright","credits"or"license"for more information.
>>>
```

The simplest program to print Hello Python can be typed and run as follows:

```
>>>print"Hello, Python!"
```

If you are running new version of Python, then you would need to use print statement with parenthesis as in **print ("Hello, Python!");**as displayed in Fig. 1.4. However in the Python version 2.4.3, this produces the following result:

```
Hello, Python!
```

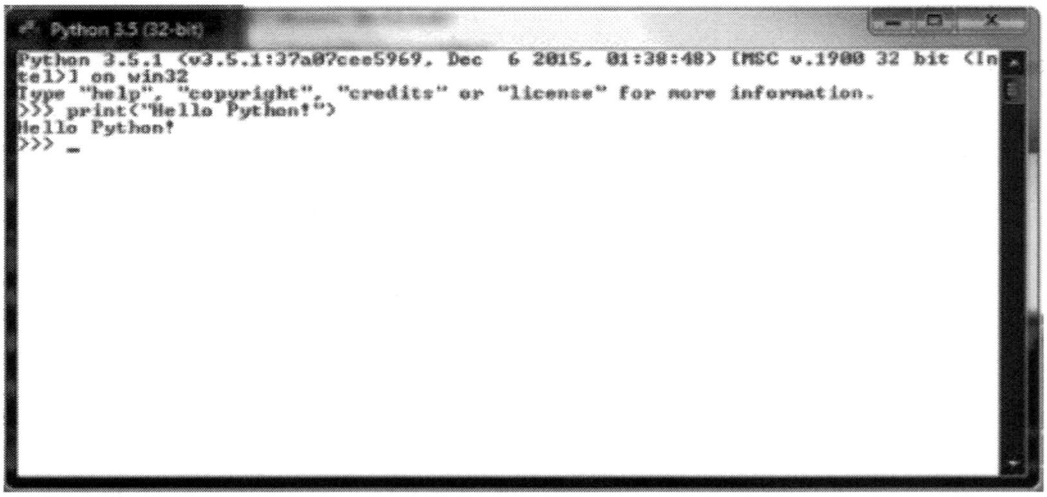

Fig.1.4. A typical Python program in the Python version 3.5.1.

1.12.2. The Script Mode Programming

In script mode programming, the complete script is written in an editor such as Notepad in Windows and then interpreter is invoked with a script parameter. It begins execution of the script and continues until the script is finished. Let us write a simple Python program in a script. Python files have extension**.py**. Type the following source code in a first.py file as shown in Code 1.1.

Code: 1.1. Illustration of Python first program (Script mode)

```
print ("Hello, Python!")
```

We have saved the script in a <prog> directory under C drive. Then at the command prompt set the path as follows and run the script by calling the python interpreter. Eventually, we will obtain the desired output as Hello,Python! The graphic representation for this method is given in Fig. 1.5.

```
C:\>prog>path %path%;c:\python
C:\>prog> python first.py
Output:
Hello, Python!
```

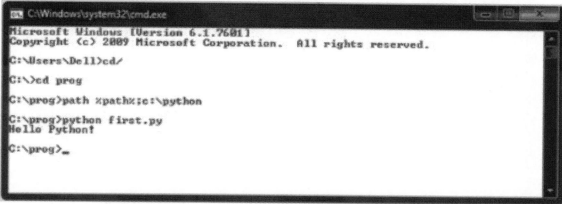

Fig. 1.5. Execution of python script file first.py

1.13. Python's Interactive Help

Python comes with built-in help utility, which is one of the major feature and support of Python language. The pre-requisite of using the built-in help of Python, you must have a little knowledge of programming. For a new programmer, it could be bit off-putting. Once, a programmer becomes familiar with programming terminology then he can make great use of built-in help provided by Python. Python programming help can be obtained in the following ways:

- Interactive mode help
- Getting help online through a web browser

1.13.1. Interactive mode help

The programmer can obtain help by running help system inside the Python interactive mode environment. The help system has its own prompt. For this, type help() at the Python prompt and you will get the help prompt (help>) with welcome message and some suggestions to get help on any module, keyword, topic, etc as shown in Fig. 1.6. Then type the name of topic you want help on such as help>import as shown in Fig. 1.7. We can see that the details of import command can be seen from the Python interface with the --more—option. Which means more information about import can be obtained by pressing space bar or Enter key.

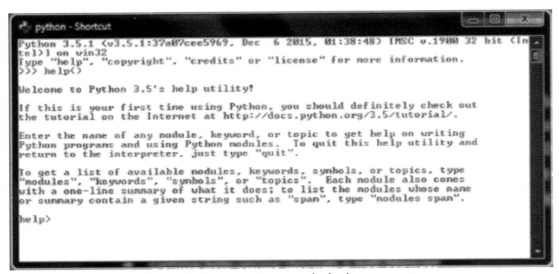

Fig. 1.6. Interactive mode help prompt

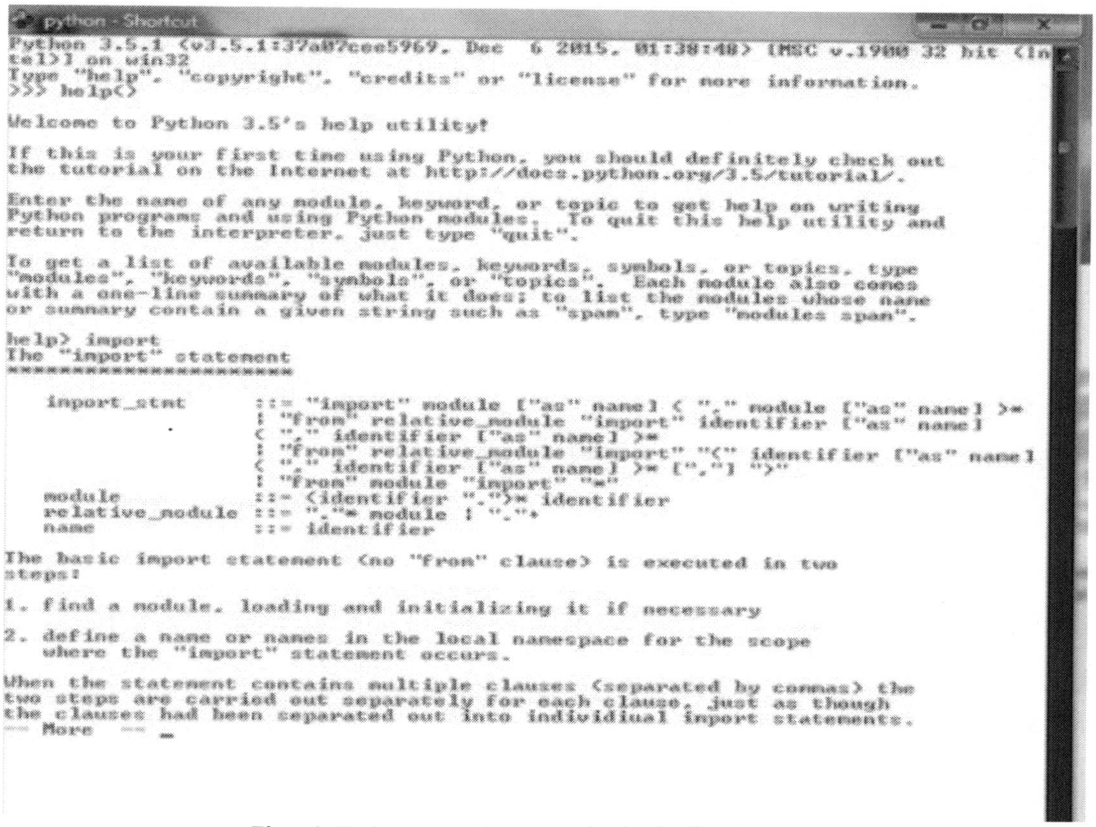

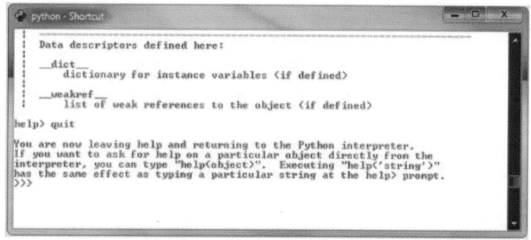

Fig. 1.7. Interactive mode help for import

The programmer can exit the help by typing the quit command at the help prompt which brings in the Python prompt again as shown in Fig. 1.8. One can obtain the Python help without leaving the Python prompt by typing help(list) at the Python prompt as shown in Fig. 1.9.

Fig. 1.8. Quitting the Python's help

Fig. 1.9. Another way of Python's help

1.13.2. Python help through a Web Browser

The programmer can obtain help online through a web browser by following the steps as under

1. Open web browser.
2. Type in the url http://www.python.org/doc/ and press Enter key.
3. This web site archives documentation for every version of Python that has been released so far. The documentation for the most recent version is available at http://www.python.org/doc/current/ .

1.14. Python differences from other languages

The Python language has many similarities to C, C++, and Java. However, there are some definite differences between the languages.

1.14.1. Difference between C and Python

C and Python are extensively used programming languages. Python is mostly used as a server side scripting language. The differences between C and Python are:

16

- C programming language was designed by Dennis Ritchie and was released in the year 1972, whereas Python programming language was developed by Guido van Rossum during 1986-1990, and was released in 1991.

- The latest version of C language is C11 and the latest version of Python programming is 3.6.1.

- In C language, indentation is not mandatory, however, in Python language indentation of code is a must.

- Data type declarations are required in C language, whereas in Python language data type declaration is not required.

- C language uses pointers on the other hand, Python language does not use pointers but associative arrays and sequences are used.

- The C language coding is complex and lengthy, whereas Python language coding is easier and short.

- C language is faster as compared to Python language.

- C language type discipline is static and weak, whereas Python type discipline is duct, dynamic, and strong.

- In C language, the variable does not increment automatically in a for loop, whereas in Python the variable used in a for loop increments automatically for the next iteration.

- The implementation of stack and queue is complex using C language, however, the implementation of stack and queue is easier in Python.

- C language supports in-line assignments whereas Python does not support in-line assignment.

- C does not support checking the array outside its allocation, however python performs checking outside array for all iterations while looping.

- In case of input/output failure, C language does not generate an error message, whereas input/output failure is supported by system calls in Python.

- C language does not support exception handling, but Python supports exception handling.

- C does not exhibit case selection library, where Python language has built in case selection library.

- Semicolon is used as a statement terminator in C. However, Python uses newline terminator and semicolon is used as expression separator.

- C does not support a garbage collection. Programmer takes care of memory management by his own. In C, Boehm Garbage collector can be used. However, Python supports mark-and-sweep garbage collection and non-moving with automatic garbage collector.

- C supports single precision and double precision complex numbers. On the other hand, Python supports double precision complex numbers.

- C language provides more safety than that of python language.

- C supports data types like char, Boolean and enum, whereas Python supports string and Boolean, and does not support char and enum.

- C supports memory management manually through malloc() and free() functions, whereas Python supports memory management through reference counting.

- C supports 8-bit, 16-bit, 32-bit and 64-bit integer and word size, whereas Python supports arbitrarily precise bignum data types.

- C supports single and multi dimensional arrays, on the other hand Python supports one dimensional dynamic size array.

- C does not support associative arrays, whereas associative arrays are used in the form of dictionaries and they are marked with curly braces.

- The syntax for accessing an array element in C language is name[index], However in Python the same syntax is used, moreover, in Python the index can be negative also. The negative number indicates the corresponding number of places before the end of the array.

- In C strcat() function is used for string concatenation, whereas in Python '+' symbol is used as the cancatenation operator of string data structures.

1.14.2. Difference between C++ and Python

Both C++ and Python are general purpose programming languages. The differences between them are:

- The C++ language paradigms are procedural, object-oriented, functional and generic, whereas Python paradigms are object-oriented, imperative, functional, reflective, and procedural.

- C++ language was developed by BjarneStroustrup in 1983 and Python was released in 1991.

- The current version of C++ is C++11, and the current version of Python is 3.5.1.

- C++ coding requires more lines of code and therefore, it is time consuming to write a code in C++, whereas Python code is 5-10 times shorter than C++ code and hence it takes less time to develop a program in Python.

- The filename extensions used in C++ are .cc, .cpp, .cxx, .h, .hpp, .hxx, and .h++, whereas the filename extensions of Python are .py, .pyw, .pyc, .pyo, and .pyd.

- The C++ language can be implemented in Turbo C++, Microsoft Visual C++, Intel C++, LLVM Clang. On the other hand, Python language can be implemented in CPython, PyPy, IronPython and Jpython.

- Python is safer language than C++.

- The C++ language has influenced Perl, LPC, Lua, Pike, Ada 95, Java, PHP, D, C99, C#, falcon, and Seed7, whereas Python has influenced Boo, Cobra, D, Go, Groovy, JavaScript, Julia, Ruby and Swift.

- C++ does not perform automatic garbage collection, whereas Python provides automatic garbage collection.

- C++ language makes use of pointers whereas pointers are not supported by Python.

- In C++ memory management is done using new and delete operators and in Python automatic memory management is done with reference counting.

- In C++ semicolon is used as statement terminator and comma as expression separator, whereas in Python newline is used as terminator and semicolon as expression separator.

- C++ supports single precision float, double, and long double data types. On the other side Python does not support single precision float, double and long double instead it supports double precision float.

- C++ supports one dimensional fixed and dynamic size array, whereas Python supports one dimensional dynamic size array.

- It is mandatory in C++ to declare type of arguments and variables whereas in Python types of arguments and variables need not be declared.

- C++ has support for associative arrays called std::map, in Python the associative arrays are termed as dictionaries.

- The syntax for accessing an array element in C++ language is name[index], However in Python the same syntax is used. In Python the index can be negative also. The negative number indicates the corresponding number of places before the end of the array.

1.14.3. Difference between Java and Python

Java is an object oriented programming language whose applications are typically compiled to byte code, which can be supported on any Java virtual machine (JVM). Python is an object oriented and high-level programming language. The key differences between Java and Python are:

- Java programming language was developed by James Gosling in Sun Microsystems and then acquired by Oracle Corporation and released in 1995. Python was released in 1991 by Python software foundation.

- The latest version of Java Standard Edition is 8 and the latest version of Python is 3.6.1.

- Java language does not compile to a native bytecode instead it compiles to a Java bytecode that can be executed on any machine. On the other side, Python language compiles to a native byte code and provides the advantages of optimization.

- Java programming includes more lines of code whereas Python programs are 3 to 5 times shorter than the equivalent Java programs.

- Java takes more time to develop and therefore slower than Python.

- In Java all variables along with their types are needed to be declared explicitly whereas no such requirement in Python.

- In Java, the data type of a variable cannot be changed whereas the data type of a variable can be changed in a Python program.

- Java is statically typed language whereas Python is a dynamically typed language.

- Java is not a compact language whereas Python is a compact language and easier to learn than Java.

- Java uses curly braces to signify the beginning and end of the block whereas white spaces are used in Python to make the beginning and end of a block.

- The Java uses automatic garbage collector to manage memory whereas in Python garbage collection is done with reference counting and supports mark and sweep garbage collection.

- Java container objects like vector and array list comprise objects of generic type. On the other side Python container objects like lists and dictionaries can comprise objects of any type including numbers and lists.

- In Java a string can not be assigned to a variable whereas Python allows a string (which once hold an integer value) to be assigned to a variable.

- In Java indentation is not mandatory, whereas in Python proper indentation is automatically enforced.

- Java does not support complex numbers, whereas Python supports double precision complex numbers.

- Java supports both fixed sized as well as dynamic sized arrays whereas Python supports only dynamic size array.

- In Java statements are terminated with a semicolon whereas Python is terminated with a newline and semicolon is used as secondary statement separator.

- Java supports signed 8 bit integer, 16 bit integer, 32 bit integer and 64 bit integer and it does not support word size whereas Python does not support 8 bit integer, 16 bit integer, 32 bit or 64 bit integer. Python supports word size int (signed).

- Every class in Java has to be defined in its own file, and in Python multiple classes can be defined in a single file.

1.15. Summary

In this chapter, we have learned about the programming language and its need. Then we have given a brief look to the origin and history of Python language along with its features and limitations. Then we have explored in detail that how Python language differs from other existing and prominent programming languages such as C, C++, and Java. The setup and installation of Python language along with a simple first program are also discussed in detail.

Review Questions

Q.1. What is a programming language? What is the need of a programming language?

Q.2. When and by whom Python language was developed?

Q.3. How will you distinguish Python language from

     a.   C

b. C++

c. Java

Q.4. Explore the applications of Python language.

Q.5. Write down the steps to install Python in the following operating systems

a. Windows

b. Unix/Linux

c. MAC

Q.6. How to execute a Python program in

a. Script mode

b. Interpreter (interactive) mode

Q.7. How one can obtain help and support of Python language? Illustrate.

CHAPTER 2

Python Data Types and Input Output

Highlights

- Keywords and identifiers
- Python statements
- Documentation and indentation
- Python data types
- Input and output
- Import

The general purpose of the programming language is to process certain kinds of data consisting of numbers, characters, and strings and to provide useful information called output. The task of processing of data is achieved by executing a set of instructions or statements referred to as a program. These instructions are formed using certain symbols and words according to some inflexible rules known as syntax rules or grammar. Every program instruction must confirm syntax rules and semantics of the language. Python language has its syntax rules and grammar, which must be followed for writing a code. In this chapter, we will discuss the basic building blocks of the language, i.e., keywords, identifiers, variables, data types, and input/output functions.

2.1. Keywords

Keywords are the reserved words in Python. A keyword can not be used as a variable name, function name or any other identifier. In Python, keywords are case sensitive. Keywords are used to define the syntax and structure of the language. There are 33 keywords in Python 3.3. The list of all the keywords is given in Table 2.1. It is to be noted that all the keywords are in lower case except True, False, and None.

and	False	nonlocal
as	finally	not
assert	for	or
break	from	pass
class	global	raise
continue	if	return
def	import	True
del	in	try
elif	is	while
else	lambda	with
except	None	yield

Table 2.1. Python keywords

2.2. Identifiers

Identifier is the name given to entities like class, functions, variables, etc. It helps differing one entity from another. You can say identifiers are the identification to a user defined variable, function or a class. Python defines certain rules while declaring an identifier, which are as follows:

2.2.1. Rules for Defining Identifiers

1. Identifier can be a combination of letters in lowercase (a to z) or uppercase (A to Z) or digits (0 to 9) or an underscore (_).
2. An identifier can not be start with a digit. For instance, 3rollno is invalid and rollno3 is valid in Python language.
3. Keywords can not be used as identifiers.
4. Special symbols such as $, &, @, #, %, etc, can not be used as identifiers.
5. Unlike C and C++, in Python, identifiers can be of any length.

| **Note** | Python is a case-sensitive language. This means, Sum and sum are not the same. It is advisable that identifier naming should make sense. While, f = 1 is valid. Writing flag = 1 would make more sense and it would be easier to determine what it performs when you look at your programming code after a long gap. Multiple words can be separated using an underscore, total_salary_of_employee. The camel-case style of writing can also be used in which every first letter of the word except the initial word is capitalized without any spaces. For example: totalSalary. |

2.3. Python Statement

Instructions that are executed by Python interpreter are called statements. For instance count=1 represents an assignment statement. while, and for are looping statements.

2.3.1. Multiline Statements

In Python language, the end of a statement is marked by a newline character. But, a statement can be continued over multiple lines with the continuation character (\). For instance,

```
sum= 10+20+30+\
     40+50+60+\
     70+80+90
```

The above statement is an explicit line continuation. In Python language, line continuation is implied inside parenthesis (), brackets [], and braces {}. For instance, we can also implement the above multiline statement as a

```
sum= (10+20+30+
      40+50+60+
      70+80+90)
```

Here, the surrounding parenthesis () do the line continuation implicitly. Similarly [] and {} can be used. For instance,

```
shape=['rectangle',
       'square',
       'triangle']
```

Multiple statements can be written in a single line as follows, where semicolon ; works as a separator

```
a=1; b=2; c=3
```

2.4. Indentation

The majority of the programming languages such as C, C++, and Java use braces {} to define a block of code, whereas, Python language uses indentation. The block of a code starts with the first unindented line. The amount of indentation is upto the programmer. Moreover, it must be consistent throughout that block. Generally, a tab of 5 white spaces is preferred. For instance, consider the code 2.1.,

Code: 2.1. Illustration of indentation in Python

```
for i in range(0, 10):
        print(i)
        if i==5:
                break
Output
0
1
2
3
4
5
```

indentation also makes the code more readable. Another instance is given in Code 2.2. as follows:

Code: 2.2. Illustration of indentation in Python

```
if True:
        print('Hello')
        a=5
Output
Hello
```

Incorrect indentation will result into IndentationError as displayed in Fig. 2.1. We can see thatcode 2.2.results in Hello whereas while making incorrect indentation an error occurs "expected an indented block" for the code given in Code 2.3.

Code: 2.3. Illustration of indentation in Python 3

```
if True:
print('Hello')
a=5
```

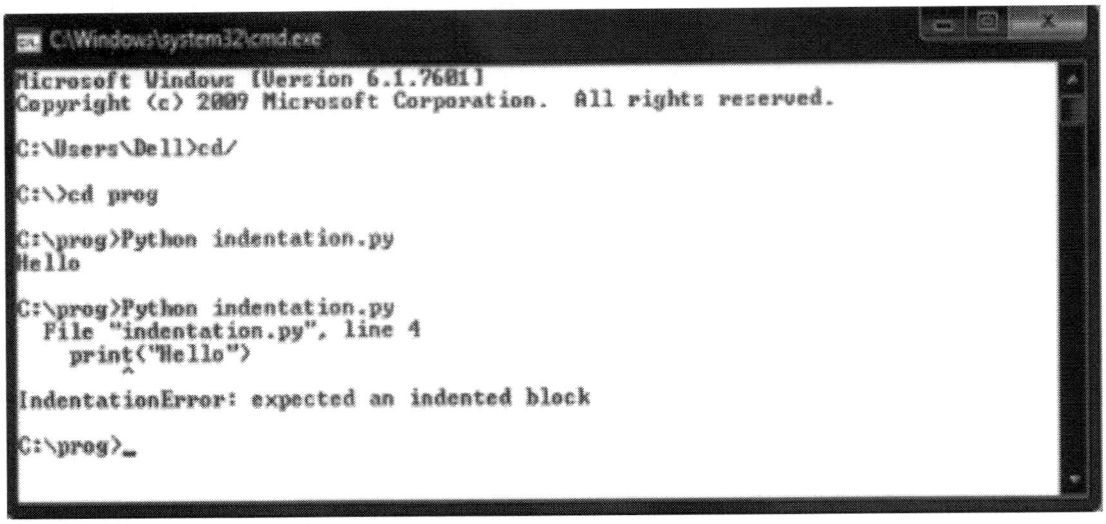

Fig. 2.1. Indentation error

2.5. Python Documentation

Documentation is a very important part of any programming language. The documentation section helps in keeping track of what is a particular line of code or a block of code is performing. It includes the details such as purpose of program, author details, important logical aspects, and date of creation. The statements within this section are called comment line in Python language. In Python language, we use hash (#) symbol to start writing a comment. It extends up to the newline character. Comments are meant for programmers for better understanding of a program. Python interpreter ignores the comment. For instance,consider the code 2.4. coded in interactive mode programming i.e., directly on the Python interpreter.

Code: 2.4. Illustration of Python documentation using #

```
>>>str = "Hello Python"
>>> type(str)
<class 'str'>
```

```
>>> print(str)       # It will print the complete string
Hello Python
>>>str[0]            # It will print the value at 0 index
'H'
>>>str[2:5]          # it will print 3rd to 5th character
llo
>>>str[2:]           # it will print 3rd to the last character
llo Python
>>>str*2             #it will print the value of str twice
Hello Python Hello Python
>>>str+"Test"        # it will concatenate Test with Hello Python
Hello Python Test
```

2.5.1. Multiple Line Comment

In some situations, multiline documentation is required for a program. In other words, comments can extend to multiple lines. This can be done by using hash (#) in the beginning of each line. For instance,

```
# this comment is
# a multiple
# line comment
```

Another way is to use triple quotes either ' ' ' or " " " for defining multiple line comments. The triple quotes include the multiple line comments. For instance,

```
" " " this comment is
    a multiple
    line comment " " "
```

2.6. Python Variables

As the name implies, a variable is something that can change. A variable is a way to referring to a memory location used by a computer program. A variable is a symbolic name for the physical location in memory and that memory location contains values, like numbers, text, etc. The variable is used to tell the computer to save some data in locations in memory or to fetch (retrieve) the data from that memory location.

One of the major differences between Python and other languages such as C, C++, and Java is that they deal with the data type. In a strongly typed language every variable must have a unique data type. For instance, if a variable type is integer, only integer values can be saved in that variable during the execution of the program. Moreover, in other languages like C, C++, Java, the variable has to be declared first before using it in the program.

Therefore, a variable is a location in memory used to store some data, i.e., a value. Variables are given unique names to differentiate between different memory locations. The rules for defining or writing a variable name are similar to the rules for writing identifiers in Python.

As explained earlier, unlike C, C++, and Java, in Python language, we do not need to declare a variable before using it. We simply assign a value to a variable and it exists. In fact, the programmer does not need to declare the type of the variable. This is handled internally according to the type of the value we assign to the variable.

Code: 2.5. Illustration of variables in Python

```
>>>a=10                  #integer variable
>>>b=34.87               # float variable
>>>c="Programming"       # string variable
```

The assignment operator (=) is used to assign values to a variable. Any type of value can be assigned to a valid variable. In the Code 2.5., it is shown that 10 is an integer assigned to the variable a. Similarly 34.87, is a floating point number and Hello is a string assigned to the variables b and c, respectively.

Another important aspect is that not only the value of a variable, but the type of a variable can be changed as well during the execution of the program. For instance, in the Code 2.6. an integer value 24 is assigned to the variable a and then a string value "hello" is assigned to the same variable.

Code: 2.6. Assigning new values to string variables

>>>a=24	#integer variable
>>>a='hello'	#string variable

2.7. Multiple Assignment

Python language, allows assigning a single value to several variables simultaneously. For instance,

```
a=b=c=1
```

Here, all three variables are assigned to the same memory location, when an integer object is created with value 1. Multiple objects can also be assigned to multiple variables as shown below:

```
a, b, c = 10, 3.5, "Jack"
```

In the above statement, an integer object with value 10 and a float object with value 3.5 are assigned to variables a and b, respectively. The string object "Jack" is assigned to a variable c.

2.8. Understanding Data Type

The type of data value that can be stored in an identifier such as variable is known as its data type. If a variable, roll_no is assigned a data value 121 that means the variable is capable of storing integer data. Similarly, if a variable height is assigned a data value 5.11, then it would be able to hold real data. In python language, every value has a data type. Since, everything is an object in Python programming data types are actually classes and variables are instance of the classes. Python language has standard data types that are used to define operations possible on them and the storage method for each of them. Python language supports seven standard built-in data types listed below:

1. **Number:** represents numeric data to perform mathematical operations.
2. **String:** represents text characters, special symbols or alphanumeric data.
3. **List:** represents sequential data that the programmer wishes to sort, merge, etc.
4. **Tuple:** represents sequential data with a little difference from list.
5. **Set:** is used for performing set operations such as intersection, difference, etc with multiple values.
6. **Dictionary:** represents a collection of data that associate a unique key with each value.
7. **File:** represents data that can be stored permanently as a document in a computer.

Now, we will discuss each data type in brief. The complete detail of Python data types is given in Chapter 5.

2.8.1. Python Numbers

Python language supports four different numerical data types as described below:

1. int : supports signed integer values.
2. long : supports long integers that can be represented in Octal and Hexadecimal.
3. float: supports floating point real values.
4. complex: supports complex numbers.

As presented above, integers, floating point numbers and complex numbers fall under Python number category. They are defined as int, float, and complex class in Python. The function *type()* can be used to determine, which class a variable or a value belongs to and the function *isinstance()* is used to check if an object belongs to a particular class.

Integers can be of any length, it is only limited by the memory available. A floating point number is accurate upto 15 decimal places. Complex numbers are written in the form x+yj, where x represents the real part and y represents the imaginary part. The creation of number objects is described in Code 2.7. (interactive mode):

Code: 2.7. Illustration of number data type

```
>>>i = 123456789          # variable i is assigned an integer value
>>>i
123456789
>>> f = 9.87654321123456789564
# variable f is assigned a floating point value
>>> f
 9.876543211234567
>>> c = 5+9j              # variable c is assigned a complex number
                          # value

>>>c
5+9j
```

Note	The output of floating point numbers goes upto 15 decimal places. So, in the Code 2.7., 9564 is truncated from the value of variable f.

To determine the type of a variable *type*() function is used as shown in the Code: 2.8.

Code: 2.8. Illustration of type() function

```
>>> type(i)
< class 'int'>
>>> type(f)
< class 'float'>
>>>isinstance(5+9j, complex)
True
```

The reference to a variable can be deleted by using the statement given in Code 2.9.

Code: 2.9. Illustration of del keyword

```
del var_name
for instance,
```

```
del i
del i, f, c
or
del var1[, var2[,var3[…,varN]]]]
deli[, f[, c[,…,
```

A few examples of numbers are described below:

int	long	float	complex
50	3682936L	4.3	5.78j
555	-0X5789L	56.28	.863j
-897	0231L	-87.32	30+29J
-1976	0XDE567AFE	-56.27e10	4.24e-8j
-936	-2467896435L	71.e19	45.j

Note	Python allows the use of lowercase l with long data type, but it is advised that the programmer should use an uppercase L to avoid ambiguity with the number 1. Therefore, Python displays long integers with an uppercase L.

2.8.2. Python Strings

Strings are identified as a contiguous set of characters represented in the quotation marks. Python language allows for either pairs of single or double quotes. Subsets of strings can be taken using the slice operation ([] and [i]) with index starting at 0 in the beginning of the string and -1 at the end or we can say that string is a sequence of Unicode characters. For instance consider Code. 2.10., where each Python statement is explained by means of comment.

Code: 2.10. Illustration of Python strings

```
>>>str = "Hello Python"
>>> type(str)
<class 'str'>
>>> print(str)            # It will print the complete string
Hello Python
>>>str[0]                 # It will print the value at 0 index
'H'
```

```
>>>str[2:5]              # it will print 3rd to 5th character
Llo
>>>str[2:]               # it will print 3rd to the last character
llo Python
>>>str*2                 #it will print the valueof str twice
Hello Python Hello Python
>>>str+"Test"            # it will concatenate Test with Hello Python
Hello Python Test
```

2.8.3. Python Lists

Lists are the most versatile and flexible compound data types of the Python language. List is an ordered sequence of items. All the items in a list do not need to be of the same type. That is a list can hold heterogeneous data types. To certain extent, lists are similar to arrays in C, C++, or Java. The major difference between array and list in Python is that all the items belong to a list can be of heterogeneous or different data types. Declaring a list is quite simple. A list contains items separated by commas and enclosed within square brackets []. Consider the Code 2.11.

Code: 2.11. Declaration of List in Python

```
>>>a=[1, 3.2, 'programming']
>>>type(a)
<class 'list'>
```

A slicing operator [] can be used to extract an item or a range of items from a list. Similar to C, the list index starts from 0 in Python. Consider the Code 2.12. to see the use of slicing operator.

Code: 2.12. Illustration of slicing operator

```
>>>a=[5, 10, 15, 20, 25, 30, 35, 40, 45, 50]
>>> a[5]                 # prints 6th value in the list
30
>>>a[0:4]                # prints 1st to 5th value in the list
[5, 10, 15, 20, 25]
>>>a[5:]                 # prints 6th to last value in the list
[30, 35, 40, 45, 50]
```

The plus sign (+) is used for concatenation and the asterisk (*) is the repetition operator. For instance, consider the Code 2.13.

Code: 2.13. Illustration of concatenation (+) and repetition (*) operators

```
>>> print a*2           # prints the list two
                        # times
[5, 10, 15, 20, 25, 30, 35, 40, 45, 50, 5, 10, 15, 20, 25, 30, 35, 40, 45, 50]
>>>b=[6, 12, 18]
>>>print (a+b)          #prints the
                        # concatenated lists
[5, 10, 15, 20, 25, 30, 35, 40, 45, 50, 6, 12, 18]
```

Lists are mutable, which means the values of elements of a list can be altered. For instance, see the Code: 2.14.

Code: 2.14. Illustration of editing list in Python

```
>>>a=[1, 2, 3]          # a is list with values 1, 2, 3
>>>a[2]=4               # a[2] is given a new value 4
>>>a                    # prints the altered list
[1, 2, 4]
```

2.8.4. Python Tuples

Tuple is an ordered sequence of items same as list. A tuple consists of a number of values separated by commas. Unlike lists, tuples are enclosed within parenthesis (). The only difference between lists and tuples is that tuples are immutable, i.e., tuples once created cannot be modified. They are used to write protect the data and they are usually faster than the lists as they cannot be changed dynamically. Tuples are defined as shown in Code 2.15.

Code: 2.15. Illustration of declaring a Tuple

```
>>> t = (7, 'Python', 2+8j)
>>> type(t)
<class 'tuple'>
```

Similar to list the slicing operator [] is used to extract items from the tuple. However, we cannot edit data into the tuple, see Code: 2.16.

Code: 2.16. Illustration of using slicing operator with Tuple

```
>>> t[1]
'Python'
>>> t[0]=8                    # altering a tuple value
#Generates error message
```

Note	Tuples can be thought of as read only lists

.

2.8.5. Python Sets

Set is an unordered collection of unique items. Set is defined by values separated by commas inside braces {}. Items in a set are not ordered. A set is defined as shown in Code 2.17.

Code: 2.17. Illustration of declaring a set in Python

```
>>> a = { 15, 20, 13, 45, 67}
>>> a
{13, 15, 20, 45, 67}
>>> type(a)
<class 'set'>
```

The operations such as union, intersection can be performed on the sets. Sets have unique values and they eliminate duplicates. See Code 2.18. for instance,

Code: 2.18. Set Illustration

```
>>> a = {1, 2, 2, 2, 3, 3}
>>> a
{1, 2, 3}
```

Since, sets are unordered collection, indexing has no meaning in sets. Therefore, slicing operator [ ] does not work on sets and generates error as displayed below in Code 2.19. and in Fig. 2.2 (interactive mode).

Code: 2.19. Illustration of using slicing operator with set

```
>>> a = {1, 2, 2, 2, 3, 3}
>>> a
{1, 2, 3}
>>> a[1]
Generates error message
```

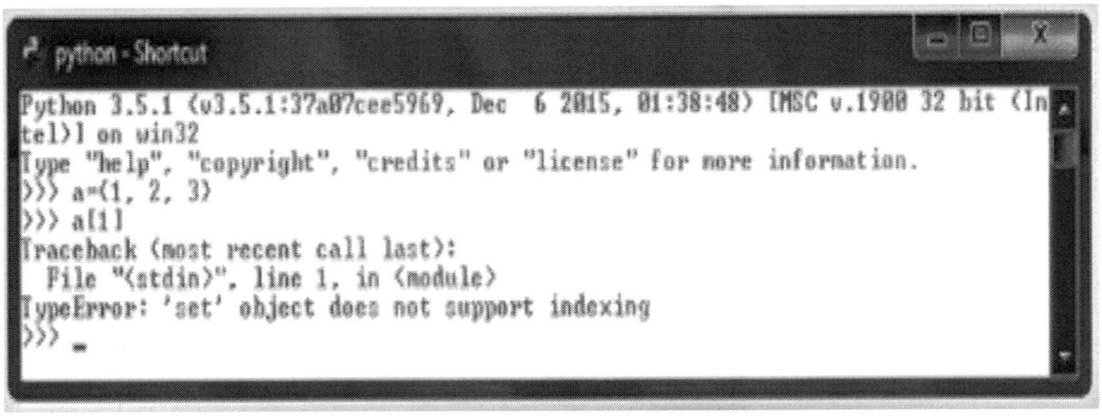

Fig. 2.2 Indexing error in sets of Python.

2.8.6. Python Dictionaries

Dictionary is an unordered collection of key value pairs. It is generally used to operate on huge amount of data. Dictionaries are optimized for retrieving data. We must know the key to retrieve the value. Python language's dictionaries are kind of hash table type. They work like associate arrays or hashes found in PERL consist of key value pairs.

Dictionary key can be of almost any Python type but usually numbers or strings. Values, on the other hand can be any arbitrary python object dictionaries enclosed by curly braces {}. The values are assigned and accessed by using square brackets []. For instance see Code 2.20.,

Code: 2.20. Illustration of Python dictionary

```
>>>dict = { }
>>>dict ['one'] = " this is one value"
>>>dict[2] = "this is numeric two"
```

Another way of using dictionary is shown in Code 2.21.

Code: 2.21.

```
>>> dict2 = { 'name': 'Smith', 'code': 1234, 'dept':'HR'}
>>>print (dict['one'])
This is one value
>>>print (dict[2])
This is numeric two
>>>print dict2
'name': 'Smith', 'code': 1234, 'dept':'HR'
>>> dict2['name']
smith
>>> dict2['code']
1234
```

2.8.7. Python Files

The file data type is used in Python to store and work with files on the computer or on the Internet. For working on a file either an existing one or a new file, it must be opened using the open() function as open("newFile"). A lot can be done on files in Python which we will learn in the Chapter 9 File Management in Python.

2.9. Data Type Conversion

While developing a program, sometimes it is desirable to convert one data type into another. In Python, this can be accomplished very easily by making use of built-in type conversion functions. The type conversion functions result into a new object representing the converted value. A list of data type conversion functions with their respective description is given in Table 2.2.

Function	Description
int(n [,base])	Converts n to an integer. base specifies the base if n is a string.
long(n [,base])	Converts n to a long integer. base specifies the base if n is a string.
float(n)	Converts n to a floating-point number.
complex(real [,imag])	Creates a complex number.
str(n)	Converts object n to a string representation.
repr(n)	Converts object n to an expression string.
eval(str)	Evaluates a string and returns an object.
tuple(x)	Converts x to a tuple.
list(x)	Converts x to a list.
set(x)	Converts x to a set.
dict(d)	Creates a dictionary. d must be a sequence of (key,value) tuples.
frozenset(x)	Converts x to a frozen set.
chr(n)	Converts an integer n to a character.

unichr(n)	Converts an integer n to a Unicode character.
ord(c)	Converts a single character c to its integer value.
hex(n)	Converts an integer n to a hexadecimal string.
oct(n)	Converts an integer n to an octal string.

Table 2.2. List of data type conversion functions in Python

2.10. Python Input and Output

In any programming language an interface plays a very important role. It takes data from the user and displays the output. One of the essential operations performed in Python language is to provide input values to the program and output the data produced by the program to a standard output device (monitor). The output generated is always dependent on the input values that have been provided to the program. The input can be provided to the program statically and dynamically. In static input, the raw data does not change in every run of the program. While in dynamic input, the raw data has a tendency to change in every run of the program. Python language has predefined functions for reading input and displaying output on the screen. Input can also be provided directly in the program by assigning the values to the variables. Python language provides numerous built in functions that are readily available to us at Python prompt. Some of the functions like input() and print() are widely used for standard input and output operations, respectively. Firstly, we discuss the output section.

2.10.1. Output

The function print() is used to output data to the standard output device, i.e., on monitor screen. The output can be generated onto a file also, which we will discuss later. The standard syntax of print() function is as follows:

print(*objects, sep=' ', end='\n', file=sys.stdout, flush=False)

In the above, objects are the value(s) to be printed, sep is the separator that is used between the values. It defaults into a space character. end is printed after printing all the values. It defaults into a new line. File is the object, where the values are printed and its default value is sys.stdout, i.e., screen. For instance, consider the Code 2.22, where 3 print statements are given. We see that first print statement prints the values of 10 20 30 40, second print statement displays the values of 10-20-30-40, with the separator -. The third print statement displays the values of 10-20-30-40# with ^ as the separator and # as the end.

Code: 2.22. Illustration of print() function

```
>>> print ( 10, 20, 30, 40)
10 20 30 40
>>> print ( 10, 20, 30, 40, sep='-')
10-20-30-40
>>> print(10, 20, 30, 40, sep='^', end='#')
10^20^30^40#
```

Another way to use print function for displaying a message on prompt is as follows:

```
>>> print (' this is an example of displaying output in Python language')
```

For displaying the value of a variable the print function is used as shown in Code 2.23.

Code: 2.23.

```
>>> a=5
>>> print ('The value of a is ', a)
The value of a is 5
```

In the second statement, we can see that a space was added between the string (The value of a is) and the value of a variable a. This is the default value of the separator.

2.10.2. Output Formatting

To make the output more attractive formatting is used. This can be done by using the str.format() method. This method is visible to any string object, see Code 2.24.

Code: 2.24.
```
>>> a = 10; b = 20
>>> print('The value of a is {} and b is {}'.format(a,b))
The value of a is 10 and b is 20
```

In the above code, the curly braces {} are used as placeholders. We can specify the order in which it is printed by using numbers (tuple index) as shown in Code 2.25.

Code: 2.25.
```
>>> print('I eat {0} and {1} in breakfast'.format('egg','sandwich'))
I eat egg and sandwich in breakfast
>>> print('I eat {1} and {0} in breakfast'.format('egg','sandwich'))
I eat sandwich and egg in breakfast
```

Another way to format the string is to use keyword arguments as shown in Code 2.26.

Code: 2.26.
```
>>> print('Hello {name}, {greeting}'.format(greeting='GoodEvening
!',name='Jack'))
Hello Jack, Good Evening!
```

Alike old sprintf() style used in C programming language, we can format the output in Python language also. The % operator is used to accomplish this as shown in Code 2.27.

Code: 2.27.
```
>>> x = 12.3456789
>>> print('The value of x is %3.2f' %x)
```

```
The value of x is 12.35
>>> print('The value of x is %3.4f' %x)
The value of x is 12.3457
```

The various format symbols available in Python are given in Table 2.3.

Format Symbol	Purpose
%c	character
%s	string conversion via str() prior to formatting
%i	signed decimal integer
%d	signed decimal integer
%u	unsigned decimal integer
%o	octal integer
%x	hexadecimal integer (lowercase letters)
%X	hexadecimal integer (UPPERcase letters)
%e	exponential notation (with lowercase 'e')
%E	exponential notation (with UPPERcase 'E')
%f	floating point real number
%g	the shorter of %f and %e
%G	the shorter of %f and %E

Table 2.3. List of format symbols in Python

2.10.3. Input

In the above, only static programs are developed in which the values of variables were defined and used in the source code. However, there must be flexibility to the user to provide his own input values at run time rather than hard code (fixed) values. To accomplish this, Python language provides *input()* function. The syntax of *input()* function is

```
input([prompt])
```

where prompt is an optional string that we wish to display on the screen as a message to the user. It is optional. The *input()* function can be used as shown in Code 2.28.

Code: 2.28.

```
>>>num = input('Enter a number: ')
Enter a number: 10
>>>num
'10'
```

Here, we can see that the entered value 10 is a string, not a number. To convert this into a number, we can use *int*() or *float*() functions as shown in Code 2.29.

Code: 2.29.

```
>>>int(num)
10
>>> float(num)
10.0
```

This same operation can be performed using the *eval*() function. As the name implies, the *eval*() function also evaluates the expressions, provided the input is a string as shown in Code 2.30.

Code: 2.30.

```
>>>int('2+3')
Traceback (most recent call last):
  File "<string>", line 301, in runcode
  File "<interactive input>", line 1, in <module>
ValueError: invalid literal for int() with base 10: '2+3'
>>>eval('2+3')
5
```

2.11. Import

It is a good practice to break large programs into modules, which makes it easy for the programmer to understand each module separately rather than the whole program at once. A module is a file which contains definitions and statements of Python functions. Python modules have a filename that terminate with the extension .py.

Alike, C, C++, and Java, the definitions inside a module can be imported to another module or the interactive interpreter in Python, where header files and namespaces are used in C/C++/Java. We use the import keyword in Python to achieve this. For example, we can import the math module by typing in import math as shown in Code 2.31.

Code: 2.31.

```
>>> import math
>>>math.pi
3.141592653589793
```

Now all the definitions inside math module are available for our use. We can also import some specific attributes and functions only, using the from keyword, see Code 2.32 for example.

Code: 2.32.

```
>>> from math import pi
>>> pi
3.141592653589793
```

While importing a module, Python looks at several places defined in sys.path for importing all the methods in that module as shown in Code: 2.33., the output for the same is shown in Fig. 2.3., which represents a list of directories.

Code: 2.33.

```
>>> import sys
>>>sys.path
```

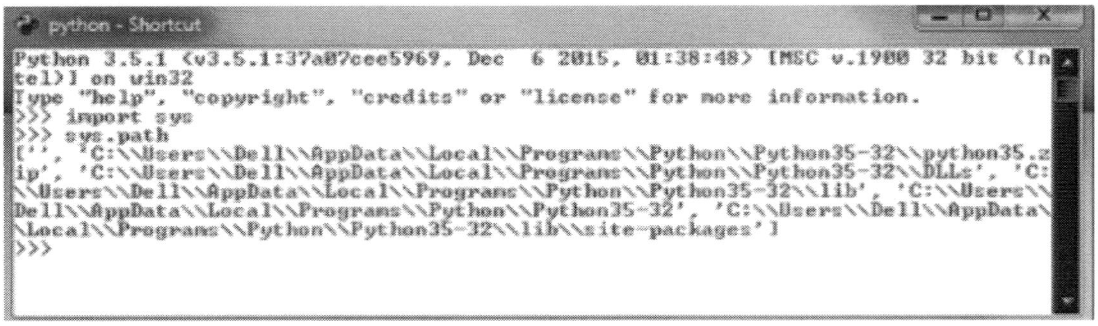

Fig. 2.3. import and sys.path representation in interactive mode.

2.12. Summary

In this chapter, we have learned basic building blocks of Python language such as keywords, identifiers, variables and the rules for using them. We have also discussed Python documentation, single line and multiline comments. After that, we emphasized on data types provided by Python language such as numbers, strings, lists, tuples, sets, dictionaries, and files. All of these data types are explained with appropriate examples. Then, we have discussed interactive input and output functions in Python. How the formatted input and output can be done is illustrated in detail. In the end, the use of import command is demonstrated that how one module can be called and used in another module.

Review Questions

Q.1. What is the role of keywords in Python language? List keywords provided by Python.

Q.2. What is an identifier? How will you differentiate it from a variable?

Q.3. What is a variable? State the rules used to define a variable in Python language.

Q.4. Why documentation is necessary in a language? How documentation can be performed in Python?

Q.5. Explain the significance of data types in Python language?

Q.6. Identify the data type that appropriately describes the data given below:
  a. 32.e10
  b. -8.56e100
  c. 34.j
  d. -876
  e. 432
  f. 4375457L

Q.7. List all the data types provided by Python language.

Q.8. How will you distinguish list and tuple data types?

Q.9. Differentiate between set and dictionary data type in Python.

Q.10. Explain all the data types provided by Python language with appropriate illustrations.

Q.11. What is a slicing operator? How can you use it? Illustrate.

Q.12. How can a user interact with the Python interpreter?

Q.13. Signify the role of input and output functions provided by Python language.

Q.14. How will you format the output in Python?

Q.15. Elaborate the significance of import command in Python with a suitable example.

CHAPTER 3

Operators and Expressions

Highlights

- All Python operators
- Precedence and associativity of operators
- Expressions

Expressions can be called as a basic sentence of a programming language. In order to construct an expression two essential entities are required which are operands and operators. Alike, other programming languages, Python also has a rich set of operators. Therefore, in this chapter, we will learn all the operators provided by the Python language. Afterwards, we will emphasize the learning of construction and evaluation of expressions by using operands and operators.

3.1. Operator

Operator is a symbol that tells the computer to perform certain mathematical or logical manipulations. Operators are used in programs to manipulate data and variables. Operators are basically used to form a part of mathematical and logical expressions. In other words, Operators are the constructs which can manipulate the values of operands. The Python language provides a rich set of operators. Python operators can be classified into a number of categories as follows:

- ➢ Arithmetic Operators
- ➢ Comparison Operators
- ➢ Assignment Operators
- ➢ Logical Operators
- ➢ Bitwise Operators
- ➢ Special Operators
  - Membership Operators
  - Identity Operators

3.1.1. Arithmetic Operators

Python language provides all the basic arithmetic operators. As the name implies, these operators are used to perform mathematical operations such as addition (+), subtraction (-), multiplication (*), division (/) and modulo (%). The arithmetic operators are listed in Table 3.1 with the description and example of each of them. The Code 3.1 (in script mode) illustrates the use of all arithmetic operators. Suppose x holds the value 40 and y holds the value 20, in the Table 3.1 except for floor division.

Operator symbol	Name	Example	Output	Description
+	Addition	x+y	40+20=60	Adds values on either side of the operator.
-	Subtraction	x-y	40-20=20	Subtracts right hand operand from left hand operand.
*	Multiplication	x*y	40*20=800	Multiplies values on either side of the operator
/	Division	x/y	40/20=2.0	Divides left hand operand by right hand operand
%	Modulus	x%y	40%20=0	Divides left hand operand by right hand operand and returns remainder
**	Exponent	x**y	40**20	Performs exponential (power) calculation on operators

//	Floor Division	x//y (if x=7, y=2)	7//2=3	Floor Division - The division of operands where the result is the quotient in which the digits after the decimal point are removed.

Table 3.1. Arithmetic Operators

Code: 3.1. Illustration of arithmetic operators.

```
# program to represent the use of arithmetic operators

x= 10
y=20
z=0

z=x+y
print("Addition is ",z)

z= x- y
print("Subtraction is ",z)

z=x* y
print("Multiplication is ",z)

z= x/ y
print("Division is ", z)

z= x% y
print("Modulus is ", z)

x=5
y=3
z=x**y
```

```
print("Exponent is ",z)

x=10
y=5
z=x//y
print ("Floor division is ",z)
```

Output

Addition is 30
Subtraction is -10
Multiplication is 200
Division is 0.5
Modulus is 10
Exponent is 125
Floor Division is 2

3.1.2. Comparison Operators

In Python programming, certain decisions are taken based on the relation between expressions or operands. For instance, we may compare the marks of two students, or the height of two persons. These comparisons can be performed with the help of comparison operators. In other words, operators compare the values of operands on either sides of them and decide the relation among them. These are also termed as relational operators. The comparison operators generate the output in terms of True (Non Zero) and False (Zero). The comparison operators are listed in Table 3.2.Suppose x holds the value 40 and y holds the value 20, in the Table 3.2. The Code 3.2 illustrates (in script mode) the use of comparison operators.

Operator symbol	Name	Example	Output	Description
<	Less than	x<y	40<20 false	If the value of left operand is less than the value of right operand, then condition becomes true.

<=	Less than equal to	x<=y	40<=20 false	If the value of left operand is less than or equal to the value of right operand, then condition becomes true.
>	Greater than	x>y	40>20 true	If the value of left operand is greater than the value of right operand, then condition becomes true.
>=	Greater than equal to	x>=y	40>=20 true	If the value of left operand is greater than or equal to the value of right operand, then condition becomes true.
==	Equal to	x==y	40==20 false	If the values of two operands are equal, then the condition becomes true.
!=	Not equal to	x!=y	40!=20 true	If values of two operands are not equal, then condition becomes true.
<>	Not equal to	x<>y	40<>20 true	If values of two operands are not equal, then condition becomes true.

Table 3.2. Comparison Operators

Code: 3.2. Illustration of comparison operators

```
# program to illustrate the use of relational or comparison operators

x = 10
y = 20
```

```
if( x == y ):
        print('x is equal to y')
else:
        print('x is not equal to y')

if( x != y ):
        print ('x is not equal to y')
else:
        print ('x is equal to y')

if( x < y ):
        print ('x is less than y')
else:
        print ('x is not less than y')

if( x > y ):
        print ('x is greater than y')
else:
        print ('x is not greater than y')

if( x <= y ):
        print ('x is either less than or equal to y')
else:
        print ('x is neither less than nor equal to y')

if( x >= y ):
        print ('x is either greater than  or equal to y')
else:
        print ('x is neither greater than  nor equal to y')
```

Output

x is not equal to y
x is not equal to y
x is less than y
x is not greater than y
x is either less than or equal to y
x is neither greater than nor equal to y

3.1.3. Assignment Operators

The special symbol = is known as an assignment operator in Python language. In general mathematics, it is used to check the equality of two operands. In Python language, it is used to assign a result of an expression or constant value to a variable. The following program Code 3.3. represents the examples of assignment statement.

Code: 3.3. Illustration of assignment operators

```
x=10          # an integer value 10 is assigned to the variable a
print (x)     # prints the value of a
```

Output
10

In the above, x = 10 is a simple assignment operator that assigns the value 10 on the right to the variable x on the left. There are various compound operators in Python like x += 5 that adds to the variable and later assigns the same. It is equivalent to x = x + 5. Compound operators are also called shorthand operators. The list of assignment and compound operators is given in Table 3.3.

Operator symbol	Name	Example	Description
=	Assignment	x=10	Assigns values from right side operands to left side operand
+=	Addition then assignment	x+=10 is equivalent to x=x+10	It adds right operand to the left operand and assigns the result to left operand
-=	Subtraction then assignment	x-=10 is equivalent to x=x-10	It subtracts right operand from the left operand and assigns

			the result to left operand
*=	Multiplication then assignment	x*=10 is equivalent to x=x*10	It multiplies right operand with the left operand and assigns the result to left operand
/=	Division then assignment	x/=10 is equivalent to x=x/10	It divides left operand with the right operand and assigns the result to left operand
%=	Modulus then assignment	x%=10 is equivalent to x=x%10	It takes modulus using two operands and assigns the result to left operand
//=	Floor division and assignment	x//=10 is equivalent to x=x//10	It performs floor division on operands and assigns value to the left operand
**=	Exponent and assignment	x**=10 is equivalent to x=x**10	Performs exponential (power) calculation on operands and assigns value to the left operand
&=	Bitwise AND and assignment	x&=10 is equivalent to x=x&10	Performs bitwise AND calculation on operands and assigns value to the left operand
|=	Bitwise OR and assignment	x|=10 is equivalent to x=x|10	Performs bitwise OR calculation on operands and assigns value to the left operand
^=	Bitwise XOR and assignment	x^=10 is equivalent to x=x^10	Performs bitwise XOR calculation on operands and assigns value to the left operand

>>=	Bitwise right shift and assignment	x>>=10 is equivalent to x=x>>10	Performs bitwise right shift calculation on operands and assigns value to the left operand
<<=	Bitwise left shift and assignment	x<<=10 is equivalent to x=x<<10	Performs bitwise left shift calculation on operands and assigns value to the left operand

Table 3.3. List of assignment and compound operators

The Code 3.4. illustrates the use of assignment operators, where shorthand operator is used with =, +, *, / and % arithmetic operators.

Code: 3.4. Illustration of assignment and shorthand operators

```
# program to illustrate the use of assignment and shorthand operator

x = 10
y =20
z =0
z = x + y
print("Value of z is ", z)

z += x
print("Value of z is ",z)

z*= x
print("Value of z is ", z)

z/= x
print("Value of z is ", z)

z=3
z%= x
print("Value of z is ", z)
```

Output

```
Value of c is 30
Value of c is 40
Value of c is 400
Value of c is 40.0
Value of c is 3
```

3.1.4. Logical Operators

The logical operators are used to compare Boolean expressions. The result of Boolean expression is always a Boolean, i.e., True or False. We can combine the results of multiple relational or arithmetic operations by using logical operators. The logical operators are logical AND (&&), logical OR (||), and logical NOT (!).

The logical AND is used when all the given conditions in an expression needs to be satisfied, while Logical OR is used when any of the given conditions needs to be satisfied. The negation operator takes only one operand and returns a false value if the operand is true and vice-versa. The logical operators are listed in Table 3.4. Let us assume the value of x=10 and y=20.

Operator symbol	Name	Example	Output	Description
&&	Logical AND	(x<y)&&(x==10)	True	If both the operands are true then condition becomes true.
		(x<y)&&(x!=10)	False	
		(x>y)&&(x==10)	False	
		(x>y)||(x!=10)	False	
||	Logical OR	(x<y)||(x==10)	True	If any of the two operands are non-zero then condition becomes true.
		(x<y)||(x!=10)	True	
		(x>y)||(x==10)	True	
		(x>y)||(x!=10)	False	
!	Logical NOT	!(x>y)	True	Used to reverse the logical state of its operand.
		!(x<y)	False	

Table 3.4. List of logical operators

The Code 3.5. illustrates the use of logical operators. In the program, only the expressions computing to true result are coded.

Code: 3.5. Illustration of logical operators

```
# program to illustrate the use of logical operator


x = 10
y = 20

if( x<y and x==10 ):
        print('true')

if(x<y or x!=10):
        print('true')

if(x>y or x==10):
        print('true')

if (not(x>y)):
        print('true')

```

Output
true
true
true
true

3.1.5. Bitwise Operators

The bitwise operators assume operands as strings of bits and the bit operations are performed on these operands. Moreover, python language allows us to operate directly at bit level using bitwise operators. As the operation is performed bit by bit, let us assume the values x=35 and y=10. Their binary equivalents are given as follows:

x   0 0 1 0 0 0 1 1

y   0 0 0 0 1 0 1 0

Now the bitwise AND, OR, XOR, ones compliment, left shift and right shift operations are performed as shown in Table 3.5.

Operator	Operation
Bitwise AND	x&y = 0 0 0 0 0 0 1 0
Bitwise OR	x|y = 0 0 1 0 1 0 1 1
Bitwise XOR	x^y = 0 0 1 0 1 0 0 1
Bitwise ones compliment	~x = 1 1 0 1 1 1 0 0
Bitwise left shift	x<<1= 0 1 0 0 0 1 1 0
Bitwise right shift	x>>1= 0 0 0 1 0 0 0 1

Table 3.5. Operations at bit level using bitwise operators

The bitwise operators are listed in Table 3.6. with x=35 and y=10.

Operator symbol	Name	Example	Output	Description
&	Bitwise AND	x&y	2	Operator copies a bit to the result if it exists in both operands
|	Bitwise OR	x|y	42	It copies a bit if it exists in either operand.
^	Bitwise XOR	x^y	40	It copies the bit if it is set in one operand but not both.
~	Bitwise ones compliment	~x	120	It is unary and has the effect of 'flipping' bits.
<<	Bitwise left shift	x<<=1	70	The left operands value is moved left by the number of bits

				specified by the right operand.
>>	Bitwise right shift	x>>=1	17	The left operands value is moved right by the number of bits specified by the right operand.

Table 3.6. Bitwise operators

As shown in the above example in Table 3.7., if one bit is moved to the left side x<<=1 using bitwise left shift operator then the outcome results in a multiple of 2, i.e., the value of x becomes 70, which was initially 35. Consequently, if 2 bits are moved to the left then the result is a multiple of 4 and so on.

On the other hand, in bitwise right shift operator, if one bit is moved to the right then the outcome is the integer division by 2. In the above example, x>>=1, results in 17 where the initial value of x was 35.

3.1.6. Special Operators

Python language offers some special type of operators like the identity operator and the membership operator. These are described below as under

3.1.6.1. Identity Operator

Identity operators compare the memory locations of two objects. They are used to check if two objects, values, or variables are located on the same part of the memory. Two variables that are equal do not imply that they are identical. The identity operators are listed in Table 3.7. Let us assume the value of x=10 and y=20.

Operator symbol	Name	Example	Output	Description
is	is	x is y	false	Evaluates to true if the variables on either side of the

				operator point to the same object and false otherwise.
is not	is not	x is not y	true	Evaluates to false if the variables on either side of the operator point to the same object and true otherwise.

Table 3.7. Identity operators

The Code 3.6. illustrates the use of identity operators.

Code: 3.6. Illustration of identity operators

```
# program to illustrate the use of identity operators


x1=10
y1=10
x2= 'Program'
y2= 'Program'
x3= [1, 2, 3]
y3= [1, 2, 3]
print(x1 is not y1)
print(x2 is y2)
print(x3 is y3)
```

Output
False True False

Here, we see that x1 and y1 are integers of same values, so they are equal as well as identical. Similarly, in the case of x2 and y2 (strings). But x3 and y3 are list. They are not identical but equal. Since list is mutable (can be changed), interpreter locates them separately in memory although they are equal.

3.1.6.2.Membership Operator

Python membership operators test for membership in a sequence. They are used to examine whether a value or variable is found in a sequence (string, list, tuple, set, and dictionary). In a dictionary, we can only test for the presence of a key, not the value. Python language provides two membership operators in and not in presented in Table 3.8. Let y=15 and x is a list with following values:

x = [10, 20, 30, 40, 50]

Operator symbol	Name	Example	Output	Description
in	in	y in x	False (0)	Evaluates to true if it finds a variable in the specified sequence and false otherwise.
not in	not in	y not in x	True (1)	Evaluates to true if it does not finds a variable in the specified sequence and false otherwise.

Table 3.8. Membership Operators

The programming example to illustrate membership operators is shown in Code 3.7.

Code: 3.7. Illustration of membership operators

```
#program to illustrate the use of membership operator

x=10
y=20
list =[1,2,3,4,5];

if( x in list ):
        print('x is available in the given list')
```

```
else:
        print('x is not available in the given list')

if( y not in list ):
        print('y is not available in the given list')
else:
        print('y is available in the given list')

x=5
if( x in list ):
        print('x is available in the given list')
else:
        print('x is not available in the given list')
```

Output

x is not available in the given list
y is not available in the given list
x is available in the given list

3.2. Expressions

Expressions form a basic sentence in any programming language. To construct an expression, we need two basic entities, which are operand and operators. As described above, Python language provides a rich set of operators. Operators in Python language are symbols, which are used to perform not only arithmetic computations such as addition, subtraction, multiplication, or division, but also logical computations. The operators specify the type of operation that need to be applied. The values that are operated on by the operators are called operands.

The combination of variables and constants along with Python operators create expressions. In other words, operators take more than one expression or operand to perform arithmetic and logical computations on it. The expressions are evaluated by using the operator precedence rules, which determine the order in which the operators in an expression are evaluated.

The precedence and associativity of operators are described in the following sections.

3.2.1. Python Operator Precedence

The precedence of an operator tells the compiler the order in which the operators should be evaluated. In case two operators with same precedence are part of an expression, then associativity is taken into consideration. The associativity of an operator tells the compiler from which side (either left to right or vice versa) the expression should be resolved.

The combination of values, variables, operators and function calls is termed as an expression. Python interpreter can evaluate a valid expression. For example consider the following Code 3.8.

Code: 3.8.

```
20-50
```

Here 20- 50 is an expression. There can be more than one operator in an expression. To evaluate these types of expressions there is a rule of precedence in Python. It guides the order in which operations are carried out. For example, multiplication has higher precedence than subtraction as shown in the following Code 3.9.

Code 3.9. (Interactive mode)

```
>>>print(20-10*5)

>>>-30
```

But we can change this order using parentheses () as it has higher precedence as shownin Code 3.10.

Code: 3.10.

```
>>>print((20-10)*5)
```

```
>>>50
```

The precedence of operators in Python is listed in the Table 3.9. It is in descending order, upper group has higher precedence than the lower ones.

Operators	Meaning
()	Parentheses
**	Exponent
+, -, ~	Unary plus, Unary minus, Bitwise NOT
*, /, //, %	Multiplication, Division, Floor division, Modulus
+, -	Addition, Subtraction
<<, >>	Bitwise shift operators
&	Bitwise AND
^	Bitwise XOR
|	Bitwise OR
==, !=, >, >=, <, <=, is, is not, in, not in	Comparisons, Identity, Membership operators
not	Logical NOT
and	Logical AND
or	Logical OR

Table 3.9. Operator precedence rules in Python

3.2.2. Associativity

We can see in the above table that more than one operator exist in the same group. These operators have the same precedence. Associativity is the order in which an expression is evaluated that has multiple operator of the same precedence. Almost all the operators have left-to-right associativity except the exponentiation which is right to left associative. For example, multiplication and floor division have the same precedence. Hence, if both of them are present in an expression, left one evaluates first. The Code 3.13. represents how an expression is evaluated in Python.

Code: 3.13. Illustration of expression evaluation considering associativity. (interactive mode)

```
>>>print(10*2//3)
>>>6.6666666666666667
>>>print(10*(2//3))
>>>0
```

Exponent operator ** has right-to-left associativity in Python and illustration is given in Code 3.11.

Code: 3.11. Illustration of associativity of exponent operator

```
>>>2 ** 2 ** 3
>>>256
>>>(2 ** 2) ** 3
>>>64
```

We can see that 2 ** 3 ** 2 is equivalent to 2 ** (3 ** 2).

3.2.3. Non Associative Operators

Some operators such as comparison operators and assignment operators do not possess associativity in Python. There are separate rules for sequences of this kind of operator and cannot be expressed as associativity. For example, a<b<c neither means (a<b) <c nor a< (b<c). a<b<cis equivalent to a<b and b<c, and is evaluates from left-to-right. Furthermore, while chaining of assignments like a= b = c is perfectly valid, a= b += 2 will result into error. An illustration is given in Fig.3.1.

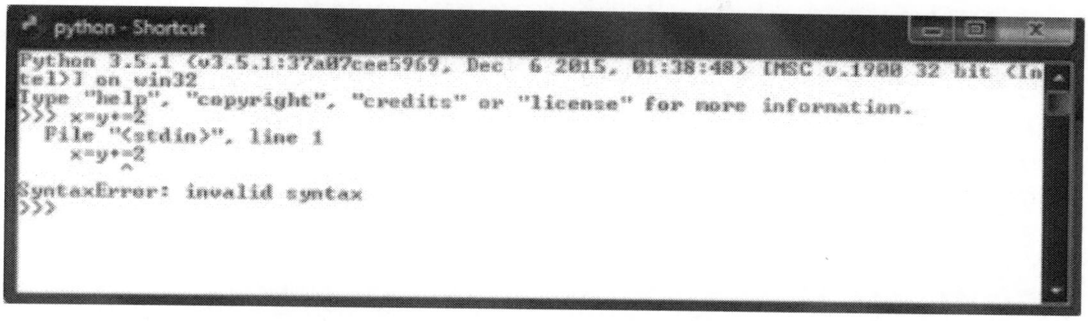

Fig. 3.1. Illustration of non associativity for the expression (x=y+=2).

3.3. Summary

In this chapter, we have learned about different operators such as arithmetic, comparison, logical, bitwise, special operators, identity and membership operators available in Python language. All the operators are described with appropriate example of each. We have learned that how operators and operands form an expression, which is the basic sentence of a programming language. The precedence decides which operator will be evaluated first and associativity decides how to evaluate an expression if two operators exhibit same precedence. Finally, we have learned how Python language evaluates expressions.

Review Questions

Q1. What is the difference between operator and operand?

Q2. List various types of operators provided by Python language.

Q3. Differentiate between assignment operator and shorthand operator.

Q4. Differentiate between the following:
   a. Division operator and Modulo operator
   b. Logical operators and Bitwise operators
   c. Relational operators and Assignment operators

Q5. What is the significance of precedence and associativity of operators?

Q6. Determine the value of each of the following expression if a=7, b=3 and c=-2
   a. b >15 && c < 0 || a > 0

b. a == c || b > a
c. a > b && b > c
d. a – b > c + a
e. a * c < = b + 11

Q7. State true or false
    a. The operators <=, >=, and != exhibit same level of priority.
    b. Associativity is used to decide which of the several different expressions is evaluated first.
    c. All arithmetic operators have the same level of precedence.
    d. Parenthesis can be used to change the order of evaluation of expressions.
    e. The expression !(x<=y) is similar to the expression *x>y*.

Q8. Which of the following expressions are true or false?
    a. 10 != 15 && !(7<12) || 34<57
    b. 10 + 10 == 20 || 2 + 6 = = 8
    c. 5 + 6 == 12 && 4 * 3 == 12
    d. 11 < 15 && 54 > 50 || 52-10 <= 42

Programming Exercises

Q1. Write a program to compute the area of the following two dimensional shapes
    a. Circle
    b. Triangle
    c. Rectangle
    d. Square
    e. Trapezoid
    f. Sphere
    g. Parallelogram

Q2. Write a program to compute volume of the following three dimensional shapes
    a. Cube
    b. Cylinder
    c. Cone

      d. Sphere

Q3. Write a program to compute perimeter of following shapes
- a. Square
- b. Rectangle
- c. Triangle
- d. Circle

Q4. Write a program to compute surface area of
- a. Cylinder
- b. Cube

Q5. Write a program to compute square of a number.

Q6. Write a program to compute square root of a number.

Q7. Write a program to compute simple interest and compound interest.

Q8. Write a program to compute total cost where number of units and price per unit are input by user.

Q9. Write a program to compute sum, subtraction, multiplication, division and exponent of given variables input by the user.

Q10. Write a program to compute distance between two points.

Q11. Write a program to compute slope of a line.

CHAPTER 4

Control Structures

Highlights

- Python if, if else, if...elif...if statements
- Python while, for, infinite loop
- Python break, continue, and pass statements

Generally, a program is executed in a sequence normally from top to bottom. The statements get executed one after the other as interpreter transfers the control from the current statement to the next statement as soon as the execution of the current statement gets over. However, in some situations the sequential flow does not work. The control needs to move to some other location in the program depending upon certain condition or there may be a requirement to execute a set of statements repetitively. Therefore, this chapter intends to emphasize on control structures which are used to alter the order of execution of a program. In this chapter, we will learn three types of control structures decision making, looping, and controlling.

4.1. Decision Making

Decision making is done with a conditional statement which allows selecting one or another execution path in a program. It causes to execute a particular block of statements after the evaluation of a given conditional expression. In other words, an appropriate action is preceded by the evaluation of a test condition to either true or false. Table 4.1. depicts a list of decision making control structures supported by Python language. Now, we will learn each of the control structure in detail.

Statement	Description
if statement	An if statement consists of an expression (which results in either true or false) followed by a block of one or more statements.
if..else statement	An if statement followed by an else statement, which executes when the boolean expression turns false.
if...elif...else statement	An if statement can be followed by an optional elif and else statements, where elif is accompanied with a test condition similar to if statement.
nested if statement	It contains if statement inside another if or else if statement(s).

Table 4.1. Python decision making control structures

75

> **Note** Python programming language assumes any non-zero and non-null values as TRUE, and if it is either zero or null, then it is assumed as FALSE value.

4.1.1. Python if Statement

The Python if statement can execute either a simple or compound statement depending on the result of the expression. The syntax of Python if statement is given as follows:

```
if test condition:
        statement(s)
```

Here, the program evaluates the test condition (expression) and will execute statement(s) only if the test expression evaluates to True. If the test expression is False, the statement(s) does not get executed. As we know that, in Python, indentation is necessary. The beginning of a block is always marked with the indented statement and the closing of a block is marked by the unindented statement. Therefore, the body of the if statement is indicated by the indentation. Body starts with an indentation and the first unindented line marks the end. Python interprets non-zero values as True. None and 0 are interpreted as False. The flow diagram of if statement is given in Fig. 4.1.

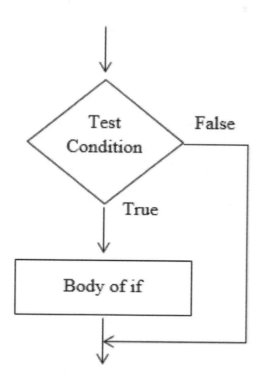

Fig. 4.1. Flow chart representing if statement

Code: 4.1 Illustration of if statement to determine whether a number is even.

```
# This program determines whether a number is even using if statement

number=input('Enter a number:')
number=int(number)
if number%2==0:
        print('Number is even')
print('out of if block')
```

Output 1:
Enter a number: 12
Number is even
Out of if block

Output 2:
Enter a number: 7
Out of if block

The programming example of if statement "to determine whether a number is even" is given in Code 4.1. In this code, number%2 == 0 is the test expression. The body of if is executed only if this evaluates to True. When user enters 12, test expression is true then the indented statement under if statement gets executed. When user enters 7, test expression is false then the indented statement under if is skipped. The unindented print() statement falls outside of the if block. Hence, it is executed regardless of the test expression. We can see this in our two outputs above. Another example of if statement is given in Code 4.2, the program code determines whether a number is positive. It is explicable from the code that if user inputs the value of number variable 5 then "It is a positive number" message will be displayed along with "out of if block" message. However, when user inputs a -5 then if statement evaluates to false and "Out of if block" message is displayed bypassing the indented statement associated with if statement.

Code 4.2. Illustration of if statement to determine whether a number is positive.

```
# This program determines whether a number is positive using if statement.

number=input('Enter a number:')
number=int(number)
if number>0:
        print('It is a positive number')
print('Out of if block')
```

Output 1:
Enter a number: 5
It is a positive number
Out of if block

Output 2:
Enter a number: -5
Out of if block

4.1.2. Python if-else Statement

The if statement executes a simple or compound statement when the test expression provided in the if statement evaluates to true. However, as in the above Code 4.1 and Code 4.2, we see that what if the test expression evaluates to false. Python language provides the solution for this by if-else statement. An else statement contains the block of code that get executed if the conditional test expression in the if statement evaluates to 0 or a false value. The else statement is an optional statement and there could be at most only one else statement following if. The syntax of if...else statement is given as under

```
if test condition:
        statement(s)
else:
        statement(s)
```

As shown in the syntax, initially test condition associated with if is evaluated, if it evaluates to true then statements following if block are executed. If the test condition evaluates to false then the statements associated with else block are executed. The flow diagram of if...else construct is represented in Fig. 4.2.

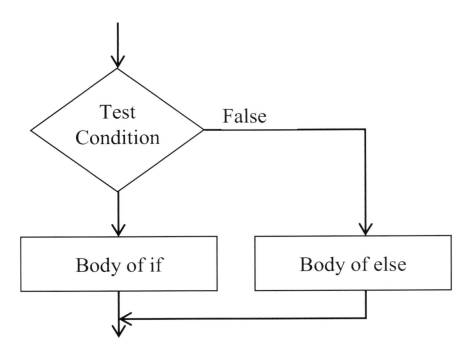

Fig. 4.2. Flow chart representing if...else statement

The programming example of if...else construct is given in Code 4.3. The program determines whether a number is even or odd. In the previous example, we see that when the test expression number%2==0 evaluates to false then "Out of if block" statement is executed. However, by using if...else construct the output is displayed as "Number is odd" for a false test condition. Similarly, in the case of another program, where it is determined that whether a number is positive or not. For a false condition the else statement block is executed, which displays "It is a negative number", as shown in the Code 4.4.

Code: 4.3. To determine whether a number is even or odd using if...else construct.

```
#This program determines whether a number is even or odd using if...else
construct

number=input('Enter a number:')
number=int(number)
if number%2==0:
        print('Number is even')
else:
        print('Number is odd')
```

Output 1:
Enter a number: 12
Number is even

Output 2:
Enter a number: 7
Number is odd

Code 4.4. To determine whether a number is positive or negative using if...else construct.

```
# This program determines whether a number is positive or negative using
if...else statement.

number=input('Enter a number:')
number=int(number)
if number>0:
        print('It is a positive number')
else:
        print('It is a negative number')
```

Output 1:
Enter a number: 7
It is a positive number

Output 2:
Enter a number: -9
It is a negative number

4.1.3. Python if...elif...else

The elif statement allows you to check multiple expressions for true and execute a block of code as soon as one of the conditions evaluates to true. It is similar to if...else if...else construct of C, C++, and Java. Similar to the else, the elif statement is optional. However, unlike else, there can be an arbitrary number of elif statements following an if. Like, if statement elif is associated with a test condition. The syntax of if...elif...else is given as under:

```
if test condition:
        statement(s)
elif test condition:
        statement(s)
else
        statement(s)
```

As shown in the syntax, If the test condition for if evaluates to false, it checks the condition of the next elif block and so on. If all the conditions are false, block of else is executed. Only one of the several if...elif...else blocks is executed according to the condition. The flow diagram of if...elif... else is given in Fig. 4.3.

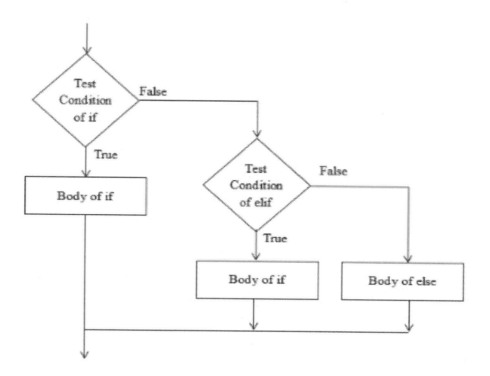

Fig. 4.3. Flow chart representing if...elif...else statement

The program representing the significance of if...elif...else is given in Code 4.5., which determines whether a number is positive, negative, or zero. It is apparent from the Output 1 that when user inputs the value of number as 5 then if condition evaluates to true and the output is displayed as "Number is positive". In the Output 2, we see that when user inputs -5 then "Number is negative" message is displayed bypassing the if and elif test conditions and in the Output 3, it can be seen that while giving input as 0, the "'Number is zero" message is displayed.

Code:4.5. To determine whether a number is positive, negative or zero using if...elif...else construct

```
# This program determines whether a number is positive, negative or zero
# by using if...elif...else statement

number=input('Enter a number:')
number=int(number)
if number>0:
        print('Number is positive')
elif number==0:
        print('Number is zero')
else:
        print('Number is negative')
```

Output 1
Enter a number: 5
Number is positive

Output 2

Enter a number: -5
Number is negative

Output 3

Enter a number: 0
Number is zero

4.1.4. Python Nested if Statements

There may be a situation when programmer wants to check for another condition after a condition resolves to true. In such a situation, the nested if construct can be used. In a nested if construct, we can have an if...elif...else construct inside another if...elif...else construct and so on. The syntax of nested if construct is given as follows:

```
if test condition:
        statement(s)
        if test condition:
                statement(s)
        elif test condition:
                statement(s)
        else
                statement(s)
elif test condition:
        statement(s)
else
        statement(s)
```

The program representing the significance of nested if is given in Code:4.6. When user inputs the value of number=5 then the condition number>=0 becomes true and control goes inside the nested if block, where it checks for number==0 test condition, which becomes false. Then else part associated with the nested if is executed and the result is displayed as "Positive number". Similarly, in the second output when user inputs number=0 then "Zero" message is displayed and in the third output, we see that by entering a negative number the outer if condition becomes false and its associated else part is executed, which displays "Negative number".

Code:4.6. To determine whether a number is positive, negative or zero using nested if statements.

```
# This program input a number and determines whether it is positive,
negative or zero using
# nested if statements

number= input('Enter a number:')
number=int(number)
if number>= 0:
        if number == 0:
                print('Zero')
        else:
```

print('Positive number') else: print('Negative number')
Output 1 Enter a number: 5 Positive number
Output 2 Enter a number: 0 Zero
Output 3 Enter a number: -10 Negative number

4.2. Python Loops

In the previous sections, we have discussed decision making statements that control the flow either sequentially or skip some statements depending upon the test condition. In some situations such as computing the table of a number, it is required to repeat some set of statements to attain the required results. This repetition can be achieved by using loop control structure. In this section, we will discuss various loops provided by Python language. We will demonstrate how loops are supportive and effective in Python language.

4.2.1. Types of loops

The repetition of a loop can also be termed as iteration, means repetitive execution of the same set of instructions for a given number of times or until a particular result is obtained. The repetition of a loop is controlled by a test expression (condition) specified with the loop. The loop begins and continues its execution as long as the test expression evaluates to true. The loop terminates when the conditional expression evaluates to false. After that, the control transfers to the next statement that follows the loop. The Python language supports 2 types of iterative or looping statements while and for as displayed in Table 4.2.

Loop	Description
while	It iterates a statement or group of statements while a given condition evaluates to true. It evaluates the test expression before executing the loop body.
for	It executes a sequence of statements multiple times until the test expression evaluates to true.
Nested loop	A loop either while or for, inside another loop is called nesting of loop.

Table 4.2. Python loop control structures

4.2.2. Python while Loop

The while loop in Python is used to iterate over a block of code as long as the test expression (condition) is true. It is also called a preset loop that is used when it is not predetermined how many times the loop will be iterated. The syntax of while loop is given as follows:

```
while test_condition:
        body of loop
```

In while loop, initially, the test expression is evaluated. If the test_expression evaluates to true only then the body of the loop is executed. After one iteration, the test expression is evaluated and tested again for true or false. This process continues until the test_expression evaluates to false. On the other hand, if the test_expression evaluates to false at the first time, the body of loop will not be executed at all and the first statement after the while loop will be executed.

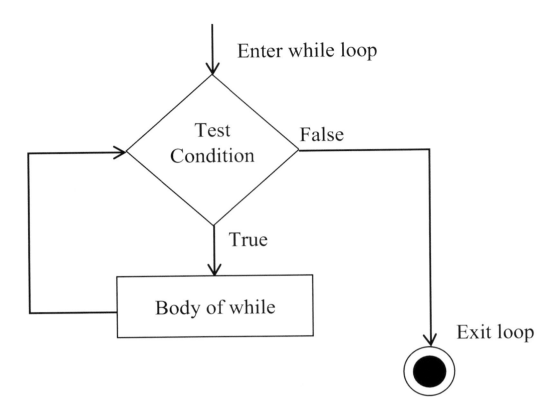

Fig. 4.4. Flow chart representing while loop

Indentation determines the body of the while loop in Python. Body starts with indentation and the first unindented line marks the end of the loop. The flow chart of while loop is given in Fig. 4.4.

Code 4.7. Illustrates a simple program to display counting from 1 to 10 using while loop. In the program it can be seen that count variable is initialized to 1 and the test_expression count<=10 evaluates to true as 1<=10. Thus, the body of loop begins execution and prints the value of count variable as 1. The count variable is incremented by 1 and becomes count=2. Then, control goes back to the test expression count<=10, that is 2<=10, which is true again and the body of while loop executed again and so on. The loop will continue to execute until the value of count becomes 11 and test expression 11<=10 evaluates to false. Eventually, we obtain the desired output.

Code: 4.7. Illustrates the use of while loop to print counting from 1 to 10.

```
# Program to display counting 1 to 10 by using while loop

count=1
while(count<=10):
        print(count)
        count=count+1
print('Outside while loop')
```

Output
1
2
3
4
5
6
7
8
9
10
Outside while loop

Another example of while is illustrated in Code 4.8. The program computes the factorial of number input by the user. We ask the user to enter a number, n. while loop is used to compute factorial of number n. The condition will be true as long as our counter variable i is less than or equal to n. We need to increase the value of counter variable in the body of the loop. This is an essential part and cannot be skipped. Undoing so will result in an infinite loop (never ending loop). Finally the result is displayed.

Code: 4.8. Illustration of while loop to compute factorial of a number.

```
# This program computes the factorial of a number input by the user

n = input('Enter n: ')
n= int(n)
i=1
fact=1
while(i<=n)
        fact=fact*i
        i=i+1
print('The factorial is:', fact)
```

Output 1 Enter n: 5 The factorial is: 120
Output 2 Enter n: 9 The factorial is: 362880

Note	The test condition and test expression can be used interchangeably as both these terms refers to the similar meaning.

4.2.3. The Infinite Loop

A loop becomes infinite loop if a condition never becomes FALSE. The programmer must be cautious when using while loops because of the possibility that the test_condition never evaluates to a FALSE value. This results in a loop that never ends. Such a loop is called an infinite loop. The programming example of an infinite loop is given in Code: 4.9. In this example since n=5, the test condition n>0 inside while remains true and therefore, the message "n is always positive" is displayed indefinite times. In such cases, the program is terminated by pressing ctrl+c altogether.

Code: 4.9. Illustration of infinite while loop.

```
#infinite while loop illustration

n=5
while (n>0):
        print('n is always positive')
print('this message will be never displayed')
```

```
Output

n is always positive
n is always positive
n is always positive
n is always positive
...
```

Note An infinite loop can be advantageous in client/server programming, where the server needs to run constantly, in order to make clients communicate with it.

4.2.4. Using else Statement with while Loop

The Python language provides a new feature, which is not available in C/C++/Java. Alike else statement with if, it can be used with the loop construct also. If the else statement is used with a while loop, the else statement is executed when the test expression evaluates to false. The following example in Code 4.10. illustrates the combination of an else statement with a while statement that prints a number as long as it is less than 5, otherwise else statement gets executed. We can see from the illustration that as long as the test condition n>0 is true the statements associated with while get executed and print the value of n as 5 ,4 ,3, 2, 1. But, when the condition n>0 becomes false the else part gets executed and the message is displayed as "The value of n is zero".

Code: 4.10. Illustration of use of else with while loop.

```
# program to illustrate the use of else with while

n=5
while (n>0):
        print(n)
        n=n-1
else:
        print('The value of n is zero')
```

Output

```
5
4
3
2
1

The value of n is zero
```

4.2.5. Python for Loop

In Python, alike while, the for loop is used to iterate over a set of statements. However, the for loop iterates over a sequence of number represented by list, tuple, string, or other sequential objects. Iterating over a sequence is also called traversing. The syntax of for loop is given as follows:

```
for val in sequence:
        statement(s)
```

If a sequence contains an expression list, it is evaluated first. Then, the first item in the sequence is assigned to the counter variable val. Next, the statements block is executed. Each item in the list is assigned to val, and the statement(s) block is executed until the entire sequence is drained out. Indentation is used to separate the body of for loop from the rest of the code. The flow diagram of for loop is given in Fig. 4.5.

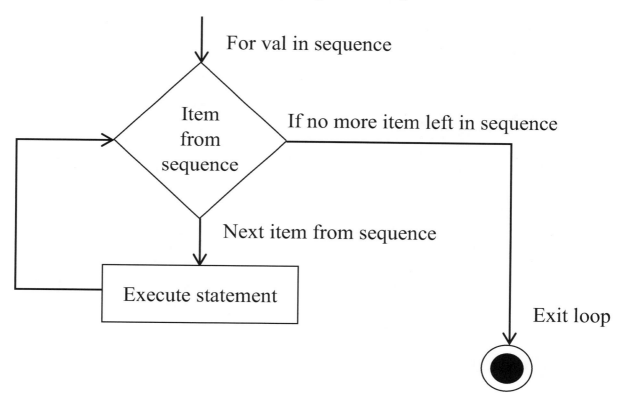

Fig. 4.5. Flow chart representing for loop

The programming example of for loop is presented in Code. 4.11. The program displays the elements of a list using for loop. Another example of for loop is given in Code 4.12., where the string values are accessed using for loop. In this program, four cities are displayed. Here, the counter variable is city, which displays the values in sequence 'cities', until the entire sequence is exhausted by for loop. One can also access the individual characters of string using for loop, which is also illustrated in the program Code 4.12., where the individual characters of PROGRAM string are displayed.

Code: 4.11. Program to display the content of marks list by using for loop.

```
# This program displays the contents of a list by using for loop

marks = [56, 43, 65, 42, 73, 51, 24 ]
for i in marks:
        print(i)
```

Output

56
43
65
42
73
51
24

Code: 4.12. Program to display cities using for loop.

```
# Program to display the string values using for loop

cities = ["Delhi", "Mumbai", "Chennai", "Kolkata"]
for city in cities:
        print('Current city:', city)

for c in "PROGRAM":

        print(c)
```

Output

Current city: Delhi
Current city: Mumbai
Current city: Chennai
Current city: Kolkata

P
R
O
G
R
A
M

4.2.6. The range() Function

The range () function is quite useful in Python programming language. It is used to generate a sequence of numbers. Most commonly, it is used with the for loop and it generates lists of arithmetic progression. The range() function can hold three arguments, start, stop and step size as range(start,stop,step size). The step size defaults to 1 if not provided. This function would be inefficient if it stores all the values in memory. So it remembers the start, stop, step size and generates the next number on the go. In the above one argument is compulsory and other two are optional as described below:

- range(12) : it will generate numbers from 0 to 11 (12 numbers). That means it generates number upto but excluding last number in the specified range. By default, it starts from 0 and goes upto one less than the specified number as shown in the example given in Code: 4.13. This argument is compulsory.
- range(2, 12): in this the sequence of numbers to be displayed starts from 2 and ends at 11. That is the first argument represents the beginning number and the second argument represents total range. To specify the first argument is optional as by default range() function starts from sequence 0.
- range(2, 20, 2): in this the third argument represents the step size which is 2, which is to be added to the current number to generate the next number in sequence upto 20. To specify the step size is also optional as by default the step size is 1 in range() function.

To illustrate the use of range() function, it is used with the list() function as shown in Code: 4.13. (interactive mode)

Code: 4.13. Illustration of range() function.

```
>>> range(12)
range(0,12)
>>> list(range(12))
[0, 1, 2, 3, 4, 5, 6, 7, 8, 9, 10, 11]
>>> list(range(2,12))
[2, 3, 4, 5, 6, 7, 8, 9, 10, 11]
>>> list(range(2, 20, 2))
[2, 4, 6, 8, 10, 12, 14, 16, 18]
```

The above statements are written directly on the Python prompt. The first statement represents the range that varies from 0 to 12. The second statement lists the values in range(12) by using the list() method. If, we specify the upper bound and lower bound in the range function then the list() method displays the values within that range as shown in the third statement. The fourth statement represents three arguments of range() method i.e., start, stop, and step size and list method displays the output as per the values provided in these three arguments.

The range() function can be used with for loop to iterate through a sequence of numbers. By accompanying with len() function, the range() function is used to iterate through a sequence using indexing as shown in Code:4.14.

Code: 4.14. Program to illustrate the use of range function in for loop.

```
# Program to iterate
# through a list
# using indexing

# List of language
language=['Python','Java','C++']

# iterate over the list using index
for i in range(len(language)):
        print("I like", language[i])
```

Output

I like Python
I like Java
I like C++

4.2.7. for Loop with else

Alike while loop, a for loop can work with an optional else block as well. The else part gets control of interpreter if all the elements in the sequence used in for loop drained out. Alike C/C++ statements if break statement is used in Python to stop a for loop then else part gets ignored. Hence, a for loop's else part runs only if no break encounters. The program to search an element from a list of numbers is given as example of this concept in Code: 4.15.

Code: 4.15. Program to illustrate the use of else with for loop.

```
# Program to show
# the control flow
# when using else block
# in a for loop

# a list of numbers
list_of_numbers=[10, 20, 30, 40, 50, 60, 70]

# take input from user
input_number=int(input("Enter a number: "))

# search the input digit in our list
for i in list_of_numbers:
        if input_number== i:
                print("Number is in the list")
                break
        else:
                print("Number not found in the list")
```

Output 1

```
Enter a digit: 50
Number is in the list
```

Output 2

Enter a digit: 100
Number not found in the list

Here, we have a list of numbers. We ask the user to enter a number and check if the number is in our list or not. If the number is present, for loop breaks with a message that number is in the list. So, the else part does not get executed. But if all the items in our list drains out then the message Number not found in the list gets printed when the program enters the else part.

4.2.8. Nested Loops

Python programming language allows to use one loop inside another loop. Following section shows a few examples to illustrate the concept. The syntax of nested for loop is as under

```
for val in sequence:
        for val in sequence:
                statement(s)
        statement(s)
```

The syntax for a nested while loop statement in Python programming language is as follows –

```
while test_condition:
        while test_condition:
                statement(s)
```

statement(s)

An advantage of nesting of loops is that we can put any type of loop inside any other type of loop. For example a for loop can be put inside a while loop or vice versa. The program Code: 4.16. computes factorials of first n natural numbers using nested for loops.

Code: 4.16. Program to illustrate nested loops.

```
# This program computes the factorial of first n natural numbers, where
the value of n is input by the user.

n = input('Enter a number: ')
n= int(n)
for i in range(1, n+1):
        f = 1
        for j in range(1, i+1):
                f = f * j
        print ('factorial of {0} is {1}'.format(i, f))
print('end of loop')
```

```
Output
Enter a number: 8
factorial of 1 is 1
factorial of 2 is 2
factorial of 3 is 6
factorial of 4 is 24
factorial of 5 is 120
factorial of 6 is 720
factorial of 7 is 5040
factorial of 8 is 40320
end of loop
```

4.3. Python Control Statements

The control statements are used to alter the normal sequence of a loop. Python language provides three types of control statements given as in Table 4.3.

Statement	Description
break	It terminates the current execution of the loop and transfers the control to the statement instantly following the block of loop.
continue	It immediately transfers the control to beginning of loop by skipping rest of the statements following it.
pass	It is used when a statement is required syntactically rather than executing any command or code.

Table 4.3. Python control statements

4.3.1 Python break Statement

Alike traditional break statement in C, the role and use of break statement is similar in Python language. The break statement is used to break the loop immediately when certain condition evaluates to true. It can be used in both for and while loop. In case, nested loops are used in a program and if break encounters in inner loop then, it terminates the inner loop and execution control goes to the outer loop. On the other hand, if break statement occurs in a single loop then it transfers the execution control to the statement immediately after the loop. The syntax of break statement is given as under and the flow diagram is displayed in Fig. 4.6.

```
break
```

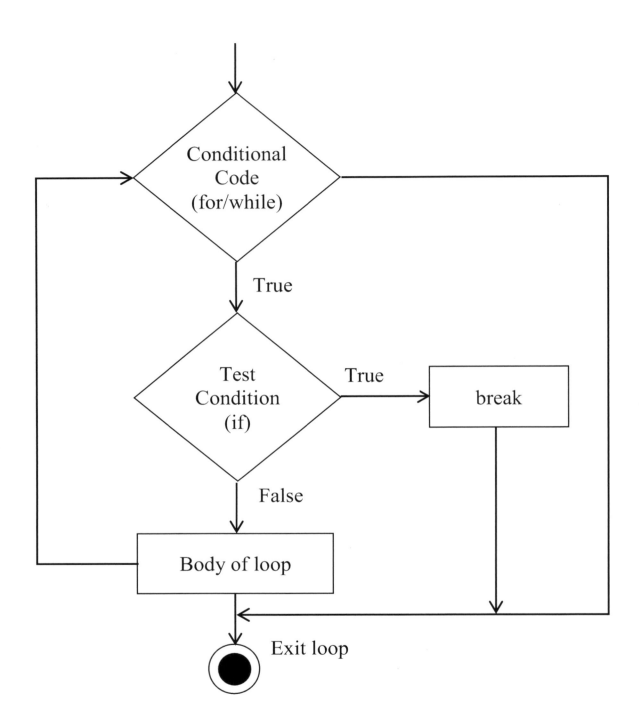

Fig. 4.6. Flow chart representing break statement

The programming example to illustrate the use of break statement in Python is given in Code 4.17. It is shown that the range of for loop is set to 0 through 9. However, when if statement encounters variable i with value 5 then break statement gets executed and transfers the control out of the loop. So, it prints 0, 1, 2, 3, 4 only and eventually "exit for" gets printed. The similar programming example is given to represent the use of break statement in while loop in Code 4.18. Another programming use of break statement has been already discussed in Code 4.15.

Code: 4.17. Program to illustrate break statement in for loop.

```
# This program represent the significance of break statement

for i in range(0, 9):
        if (i==5):
                break
        print(i)
print('exit for')
```

Output:

0

1

2

3

4

exit for

Code: 4.18. Program to illustrate break statement in while loop.

```
# This program represents the use of break statement in while loop

count=1
while(count<=10):
        if(count == 5):
                break
        print(count)
        count=count+1
print('exit while')
```

Output:

```
0
1
2
3
4
exit while
```

4.3.2. Python continue Statement

The continue statement returns the control to the beginning of the loop. It overpasses (skips) all the remaining statements in the current iteration of the loop and moves the control back to the top of the loop. It can be used with both while as well as for loop. The syntax of continue statement is given as under and the flow diagram is displayed in Fig. 4.7.

```
continue
```

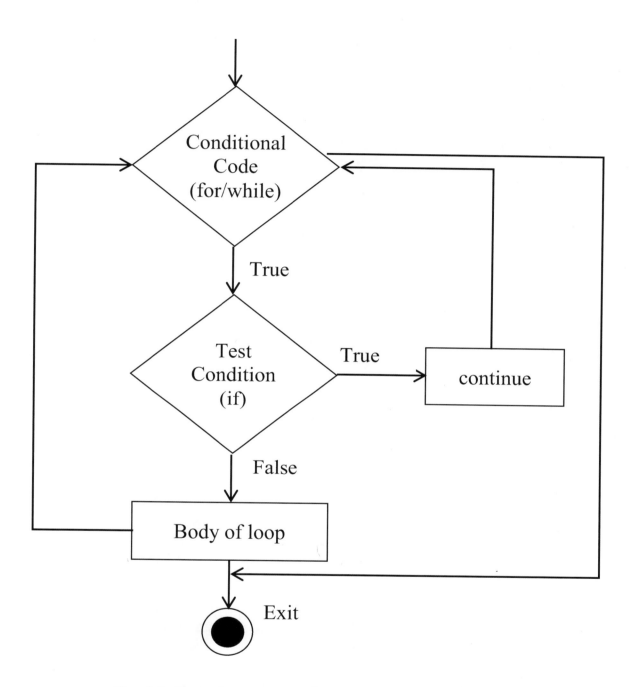

Fig. 4.7. Flow chart representing continue statement

The programming example of continue control statement is given in Code: 4.19. This program is same as the above example except the break statement has been replaced with continue. The program continue with the loop, if the value of i=5. We see that the execution control moves back to the beginning of the loop when i=5 triggers and skips rest of the statements. Thus, we see in the output that all the digits up to 9 get printed except 5.

Code: 4.19. Program to illustrate the use of continue statement.

```
# This program represent the significance of continue statement

for i in range(0, 9):
        if (i==5):
                continue
        print(i)
print('exit for')
```

```
Output:

0
1
2
3
4
6
7
8
9
exit for
```

4.3.3. Python pass Statement

Unlike C, C++, Java, Python language provides a new statement pass. The pass statement is principally represents a null operation, which means nothing happens when it executes. It can be used when certain statement is required only syntactically but programmer does not wish to execute any code or command.

The pass is valuable in situations, when programmer wish to write certain code at a later stage within the loop to perform some action. The syntax of pass statement is given as under

```
pass
```

The programming example of pass statement is given in Code: 4.20. In this program pass statement is used inside for loop. The program prints all the digits from 0 to 9. However, when i=5 condition becomes true then pass statement gets executed and it prints This is a pass statement.

| Note | The difference between Python comment and pass is that the comments are entirely ignored by the interpreter but pass is not ignored. |

Code: 4.20. Program to illustrate the use of pass statement.

```
# This program represents the significance of pass statement

for i in range(0, 9):
        if (i==5):
                pass
                print('This is a pass statement')
        print(i)
print('Exit for')
```

```
Output
0
1
2
3
4
This is a pass statement
5
6
7
8
9
Exit for
```

4.4. Summary

In this chapter, we have learned all the control structures provided by Python language. The decision making statement if, if else, elif, nested if are elaborated thoroughly. The most likely used looping constructs while and for are discussed with appropriate programming example of each. The new features of Python while loop with else, for loop with else, and range() function are explained with their instances. Other control statements such as break, continue, and pass are also discussed. The flow diagrams of all the control structures are also given.

Review Questions

Q1. What do you understand by control statements?

Q2. Describe decision making control statements of Python with example of each.

Q3. Differentiate between the following
   a. if and if else
   b. if...elif...else and nested if

Q4. Differentiate between break, continue, and pass statements.

Q5. Write an appropriate programming code to demonstrate the difference between break and continue.

Q6. What is meant by looping? Describe two different forms of looping constructs of Python language.

Q7. How while loop differs from for loop? Give example.

Q8. Illustrate the purpose of else with for loop.

Q9. Illustrate the purpose of else with while loop.

Q10. What is the significance of range() function in for loop?

Q11. Why len() function is used with for loop?

Q12. What do you understand by nesting of loops? Can one type of loop be embedded inside another loop.

Q13. Draw the flow control diagrams of the following
   a. if
   b. if-else
   c. if...elif...else
   d. while
   e. for
   f. break

g. continue

Q14. When while loop is preferred over for loop? Give example.

Programming Exercises

1. Write a program to print largest of three numbers using if-else statement.
2. Write a program to determine whether a year is leap or not.
3. Write a program to determine whether a number is even or odd.
4. Write a program to determine whether a triangle is isosceles or not?
5. Write a program to find out the roots of a quadratic equation.
6. Write a program to print numbers upto N which are not divisible by 3, 6, and 9, e.g., 1, 2, 4, 5, 7, ...
7. Write a program that will read the value of x and evaluate the following function

$$R(p) = \begin{cases} 1 & p = 0 \\ 2\cos(\pi p) & p > 0 \\ 2\sin(\pi p) & p < 0 \end{cases}$$

8. Write a program to print multiplication table.
9. Write a program to compute sum of first n natural numbers.
10. Write a program that prompts a number from the user and generates the Fibonacci sequence upto that number. The Fibonacci sequence is given as under:
    0 1 1 2 3 5 8 13 21 43 ...
11. Write a program that prompts the user for an integer number and then prints all its factors.
12. Write a program to determine whether a number is palindrome or not.
13. Write a program to determine whether a number is prime or not.
14. Write a program to determine an Armstrong number.
15. Write a program to reverse the digits of a number.
16. Write a program to compute HCF of a number input by the user.
17. Write a program to read n integer numbers interactively and print the biggest and smallest numbers.

18. Write a program that input data for a Python list. Then compute and print the sum and average of entered numbers.
19. Write a program to input 10 numbers. Then compute and display the sum of even numbers and product of odd numbers.
20. Write a program to count the occurrence of a digit 5 in a given integer number.
21. Write a program to compute the factorial of a number.
22. Write a program to generate prime numbers in a certain range input by the user.
23. Write a program to calculate and display Geometric and Harmonic means.
24. Write a program to convert a decimal number into its binary equivalent and vice versa.
25. Write program to evaluate the following expressions

    a. $$x - \frac{x^3}{3!} + \frac{x^5}{5!} - \frac{x^7}{7!} + ... \frac{x^n}{n!}$$

    b. $$x - \frac{x^2}{2!} + \frac{x^3}{3!} - \frac{x^4}{4!} + ... \frac{x^n}{n!}$$

26. Write a program to print all the possible combinations of 4, 5, and 6.

CHAPTER 5

Python Native Data Types

Highlights

- Python native data types
- Number
- List, tuple, set, dictionary
- Strings

As described in Chapter 2, Python language supports different data types to handle various sort of data. Here in this chapter, we describe the following Python native data types in detail.

Number: represents numeric data to perform mathematical operations.
String: represents text characters, special symbols or alphanumeric data.
List: represents sequential data that the programmer wishes to sort, merge, etc.
Tuple: represents sequential data with a little difference from list.
Set: is used for performing set operations such as intersection, difference, etc with multiple values.
Dictionary: represents a collection of data that associate a unique key with each value.

5.1. Number

Number is an object in Python, and it is created when some value is assigned to it. Number data type is used to hold numerical data. Python language supports four different numeric data types as described below:

- **int (signed integers)**: Alike C/C++/Java, Python supports integer numbers, which are whole numbers positive as well as negative having no decimal point.

- **long (long integers)**: Similar to integers but with limitless size. In Python long integers are followed by a lowercase or uppercase L.

- **float (floating point real values)** : Alike C/C++/Java, Python supports real numbers, called as floats. These number are written with a decimal point or sometimes in a scientific notation, with exponent e such as 5.9e7 i.e. 5.9×10^7, where e represents the power of 10.

- **complex (complex numbers)** : Unlike C/C++/Java, Python supports complex data type. It holds complex numbers of the form x+iy, where x and y are floating point numbers and i is iota representing the square root of -1 (imaginary number). Complex numbers have two parts where x is known as the real part and y is called the imaginary part as it is with iota.

Unlike C/C++/Java, in Python the variable declaration is not mandatory. The programmer just assign the value to a variable and that variable exists with the data type based on the value assigned. For example, the Code: 5.1 (interactive mode) represents, an illustration of number data type that how a variable holds certain type of data and it exists.

Code: 5.1. Illustration of number data type.

```
>>>i = 123456789              # variable i is assigned an
integer value
>>>i
123456789
>>> f = 9.8765432112345679564  # variable f is assigned a floating
                               #point value
>>> f
 9.876543211234567
>>> c = 5+9j                   # variable c is assigned a
                               #complex number value
>>>c
5+9j
```

The data type determination, reference deletion, and different types of numbers are already discussed in Chapter 2 under Section 2.8.1.

5.1.1. Number Type Conversion

Python has the in-built feature to convert the data types of an expression containing different data types in to a common type for evaluation. However, in order to fulfill the requirements of an operator or a function argument, sometimes the programmer needs to convert a data type to another type forcibly. This can be achieved by type conversion functions as listed Table 5.1.

Conversion function	Role
int(x)	converts x to a plain integer
long(x)	converts x to a long integer
float(x)	converts x to a floating-point number
complex(x)	converts x to a complex number with real part x and imaginary part zero

complex(x, y)	converts x and y to a complex number with real part x and imaginary part y. where, x and y are numeric expressions

Table 5.1. Python type conversion functions

5.1.2. Python Mathematical Functions

Since we are working on numbers, Python language contains a rich set of built-in mathematical, and trigonometric, and random number functions, which operate on numbers input by the user. The mathematical functions are listed in Table 5.2. with description of each of them. The programming example, representing the use of mathematical functions is given in Code: 5.2. The programmer needs to import math namespace for executing mathematical functions.

Mathematical function	Computes/Returns
abs(x)	The absolute value of x, which is positive value
fabs(x)	The absolute value of x
sqrt(x)	The square root of x, where x>0
pow(x, y)	The value of x^y
ceil(x)	The smallest integer not less than x
floor(x)	The largest integer not greater than x
round(x, [n])	x rounded to n digits from the decimal point.
exp(x)	Exponent of x, i.e., e^x
log(x)	The natural logarithm of x, where x>0
log10(x)	The base-10 logarithm of x, where x>0
cmp(x, y)	0 if x==y, -1 if x<y, and 1 if x>y, (compares the values of x and y)
modf(x)	The fractional and integer parts of x in a two-item tuple. Both parts have the same sign as x. The integer part is returned as a float
max(x1, x2, ...)	The largest value among its parameters
min(x1, x2, ...)	The smallest value among its parameters

Table 5.2. List of Python mathematical functions

Code: 5.2. Programming illustration of Python mathematical functions.

```
# This program represents the use of Python mathematical functions

import math

x=-10.5
y=abs(x)
print('abs(x)={0}'.format(y))

x=9.5
y=math.fabs(x)
print('fabs(x)={0}'.format(y))

x=256
y=math.sqrt(x)
print('sqrt(x)={0}'.format(y))

x=2
y=16
z=math.pow(x, y)
print('pow({0}, {1})={2}'.format(x,y,z))

x=4.31
y=math.ceil(x)
print('ceil(x)={0}'.format(y))

x=4.31
y=math.floor(x)
print('floor(x)={0}'.format(y))

x=10.5628468
y=round(x, 3)
print('round({0}, 3)={1}'.format(x, y))

x=2
y=math.exp(x)
print('exp(x)={0}'.format(y))

x=20
y=math.log(x)
```

```
print('log(x)={0}'.format(y))

x=20
y=math.log10(x)
print('log10(x)={0}'.format(y))

x=10
y=20
z=cmp(x,y)
print('cmp({0}, {1})={2}'.format(x, y, z))

x=12.4354683
y=math.modf(x)
print('modf(x)={0}'.format(y))

y=max(-10, 23, 54, 21, 0)
print('max(-10, 23, 54, 21, 0)={0}'.format(y))

y=min(-10, 23, 54, 21, 0)
print('min(-10, 23, 54, 21, 0)={0}'.format(y))
```

```
Output:
abs(x)=10.5
fabs(x)=9.5
sqrt(x)=16.0
pow(2, 16)=65536.0
ceil(x)=5
floor(x)=4
round(10.5628468, 3)=10.563
exp(x)=7.38905609893065
log(x)=2.995732273553991
log10(x)=1.3010299956639813
cmp(10, 20)= -1
modf(x)=(0.43546830000000014, 12.0)
max(-10, 23, 54, 21, 0)=54
min(-10, 23, 54, 21, 0)=-10
```

Note	Mathematical functions abs(), round(), and cmp() do not require to import math namespace.

5.1.3. Python Trigonometric Functions

Python language provides a set of trigonometric functions listed in Table 5.2. with the description of each. The programming code to characterize the use of trigonometric functions is given in Code: 5.3.

Trigonometric function	Returns
sin(x)	Sine of x in radians
cos(x)	Cosine of x in radians
tan(x)	Tangent of x in radians
asin(x)	Arc sine of x in radians
acos(x)	Arc cosine of x in radians
atan(x)	Arc tangent of x in radians
atan2(y, x)	Atan(y/x) in radians
degrees(x)	Converts an angle x from radians to degrees
radians(x)	Converts an angle x from degrees to radians
hypot(x, y)	Computes the Euclidean distance, i.e., sqrt(x*x+y*y)

Table 5.3. Python trigonometric functions

Code: 5.3. Programming illustration of Python trigonometric functions.

```
# This program illustrates the use of trigonometric functions

import math

x=30
y=math.radians(x)
print('radians({0})={1}'.format(x, y))


x=1.57
y=math.degrees(x)
```

```
print('degrees({0})={1}'.format(x, y))

x=0.5235987755982988
y=math.sin(x)
print('sin({0})={1}'.format(x, y))

x=0.5235987755982988
y=math.cos(x)
print('cos({0})={1}'.format(x, y))

x=0.5235987755982988
y=math.tan(x)
print('tan({0})={1}'.format(x, y))

x=0.5235987755982988
y=math.asin(x)
print('asin({0})={1}'.format(x, y))

x=0.5235987755982988
y=math.acos(x)
print('acos({0})={1}'.format(x, y))

x=0.5235987755982988
y=math.atan(x)
print('atan({0})={1}'.format(x, y))

x=3
y=4
z=math.atan2(y, x)
print('atan2({0}, {1})={2}'.format(x, y, z))

x=3
y=4
z=math.hypot(x, y)
print('hypot({0}, {1})={2}'.format(x, y, z))
```

```
Output:

radians(30)=0.5235987755982988
degrees(1.57)=89.95437383553924
sin(0.5235987755982988)=0.49999999999999994
cos(0.5235987755982988)=0.8660254037844387
tan(0.5235987755982988)=0.5773502691896257
asin(0.5235987755982988)=0.5510695830994463
acos(0.5235987755982988)=1.0197267436954502
atan(0.5235987755982988)=0.48234790710102493
atan2(3, 4)=0.9272952180016122
hypot(3, 4)=5.0
```

5.1.4. Python Random Number Functions

Random numbers are very useful in numerous computer science problems such as simulators, games, security, privacy, testing applications, etc. Python language provides a set of random number functions to handle various computer science problems as described above. The list of random number functions is given in Table 5.4. The programmer needs to import random module before calling any of the random number function. The programming example, representing the use of random number functions is given in Code 5.4.

Random number function	Returns
random()	A random number r such that, $0 \le r \le 1$
uniform(x, y)	The random float r such that $x \le r \le y$
seed(x)	It sets the starting integer value used in generating random numbers. This function is called before calling any other random number function.
choice(seq)	A random item from a string, list, or tuple
shuffle(list)	Randomizes the items in a list.
randrange(start, stop, step)	A randomly selected item from a specified range.

Table 5.4. List of random number functions

Code: 5.4 Programming illustration of Python random number functions.

```python
# This program illustrates the use of trigonometric functions

import random

r1=random.random()
print("random number 1={0}".format(r1))

r2=random.random()
print("random number 2={0}".format(r2))

r1=random.uniform(10, 20)
print("uniform random number 1={0}".format(r1))

r1=random.uniform(10, 20)
print("uniform random number 2={0}".format(r1))

random.seed(15)
r1=random.random()
print("random number with seed 15={0}".format(r1))

list=[70, 20, 30, 40, 50]
r1=random.choice(list)
print("uniform random number 1={0}".format(r1))

str='Hello Python'
r1=random.choice(str)
print("uniform random number from string={0}".format(r1))

list=[70, 20, 30, 40, 50]
r1=random.shuffle(list)
print("shuffled list={0}".format(list))

r1=random.randrange(10, 100, 3)
print("random number from a range={0}".format(r1))

r1=random.randrange(10, 100, 4)
print("random number from a range={0}".format(r1))
```

Output:

random number 1=0.1113694067277533
random number 2=0.2822991673774605
uniform random number 1=18.907430735664263
uniform random number 2=10.620373343283184
random number with seed 15=0.965242141552123
uniform random number 1=70
uniform random number from string=t
shuffled list=[40, 30, 50, 20, 70]
random number from a range=13
random number from a range=94

5.1.5. Python Mathematical Constants

Unlike, C/C++/Java, Python language provides built in mathematical constants pi and e, which exhibit fixed values while performing mathematical computations. A program to illustrate mathematical constants is given in Code 5.5. Note that, the programmer requires to import math module for fetching the values of pi and e.

Code: 5.5 Programming illustration of Python mathematical constants.

```python
# Representation of mathematical constants pi and e

import math

print('pi={0}'.format(math.pi))
print('e={0}'.format(math.e))
```

Output:

pi=3.141592653589793
e=2.718281828459045

5.2. Python Lists

In Python, the most basic data structure is the list. List is similar to array as in C, C++, or Java, since the index of first element of list is zero, second element is one, and so on. However, the list is a collection of heterogeneous data elements. That means a list can contain numeric as well as character data.

Various sort of operations can be performed on lists. These include indexing, slicing, adding, multiplying, and checking for membership. We will present all these operations through illustrations in the following sections. Apart from that, Python language also contains various built-in functions, we will discuss them as well.

5.2.1. Creating a List

It is very simple to create lists in Python. All you need to do is to place all the comma separated elements inside a square bracket []. The list can contain any number of elements of different data types (integer, float, character, etc). Moreover, a list can contain another list and it is referred to as nested list. The Code 5.6. illustrates the creation of a list. In this program, we see that three lists are created. The first list name is new_list, which is a simple list with homogeneous data elements. The second list new_list1, represents collection of heterogeneous data elements, and the third list new_list2, represents nested list. The output can be verified in the output section.

Code: 5.6. Illustration of creating a list.

```
#Illustration of creating a list

new_list=[1, 2, 3, 4]            # Homogeneous data elements
print(new_list)

new_list1=[1, "John", 55.5]      # Heterogeneous data elements
print(new_list1)

new_list2=[111, [1, "Clara", 75.5]]      # Nested list
print(new_list2)
```

Output

```
[1, 2, 3, 4]
[1, 'John', 55.5]
[111, [1, 'Clara', 75.5]]
```

5.2.2. Traversing a List

Traversing refers to accessing or visiting elements of a list. The Python language provides different ways in which we can access the elements of a list. These are indexing, negative indexing and slicing. We discuss each of them with programming illustrations.

5.2.2.1. Indexing

As in other languages, such as C, C++, & Java, the index of elements of a list starts from 0. Therefore, if a list contain 10 elements then its index will vary from 0 to 9. If user tries to access an element from a list beyond the range will result into an IndexError. Apart from that, the index of a list is always an integer number. If user tries to access a list element using floating point indexing, will result in TypeError. In order to access the list elements, the indexing operator also called subscript operator [] is used. The programming illustration of accessing elements of a list is given in Code 5.7. In the program a datalist with five elements is created. Then, the elements 0, 2, and 4 of the list are displayed by using the index operator [].

Code: 5.7. Illustration of list traversal.

```
#Illustration of traversing a list

datalist=[23, 45, 31, 53, 62]
print(datalist[0])
print(datalist[2])
print(datalist[4])
```
Output

```
23
31
62
```

Another programming example of traversing is given in Code 5.8., in which we see that while accessing list element beyond its range results into an error. In this program, we see that the element at index 5 is accessed. Since, the datalist contains 5 elements with index 0 to 4. Therefore, accessing the value at index 5 results into an IndexError as shown in the output.

Code: 5.8. IndexError illustration.

```
#Illustration of traversing a list beyond range

datalist=[23, 45, 31, 53, 62]
print(datalist[5])
```

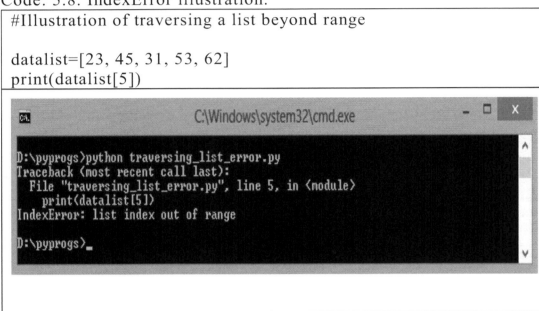

5.2.2.2. Traversing Nested Lists

By using the index operator the nested list can also be traversed very easily. The illustration for the same is given in Code 5.9. In this program, we see that two nested lists are created as member of the datalist. The first nested list is at location index 1 and other is at location index 2. Therefore, the name elements John and Sandra of these nested lists are accessed as datalist[1][1], and datalist[2][1].

Code: 5.9. Illustration of traversal of a nested list.

```
#Illustration of traversing a nested list

datalist=[1, [1001, "John", 45.5], [1002, "Sandra", 56.5]]
```

```
print(datalist[1][1])
print(datalist[2][1])
```

Output

John
Sandra

5.2.2.3. Negative Indexing

The Python language also allows negative indexing. However, this features is not available in other languages C, C++, and Java. The index of -1 refers to the last elements of the list, the index -2 refers to second last element and so forth. The illustration for the same is given in Code 5.10. However, if the indexing goes beyond range then IndexError occurs as list index out of range.

Code: 5.10. Illustration of negative indexing.

```
#Illustration of traversing a list using negative indexing

datalist=[23, 45, 31, 53, 62]
print(datalist[-1])
print(datalist[-3])
print(datalist[-5])
```

Output

62
31
23

5.2.2.4. Slicing

The slicing operator is used to access the list elements within a specific range. The symbol of slicing operator is colon (:). The programming representation for understanding the concept is given in Code: 5.11. In this program, we create a datalist with five elements. The slicing operator is used with different ranges positive as well as negative indexing. The first range is set to be 0:3 that means the elements with index value 0 through 2 will be displayed. It is to be noted that in the syntax of slicing operator [beg:end], the end is excluded from the range. Thus, the datalist[0:3] results into [23, 45, 31]. Similarly, for the other examples. The just [:] displays all the elements of a list from beginning to end.

Code: 5.11. Illustration of slicing operator.

```
#Illustration of slicing operator

datalist=[23, 45, 31, 53, 62]
print(datalist[0:3])
print(datalist[2:4])
print(datalist[:-4])
print(datalist[-4:])
print(datalist[:])
```

```
Output

[23, 45, 31]
[31, 53]
[23]
[45, 31, 53, 62]
[23, 45, 31, 53, 62]
```

5.2.3. Changing or Adding Elements to a List

As we know that lists are mutable. That means the elements of a list can be changed or new elements can be added into a list. The process can be performed with the help of assignment operator (=). The programming example representing the updating elements in a list is given in Code 5.12. In this program, we see that the value of third element of the datalist is changed to 60 and the value of fifth element is changed to 12. This is performed very easily by using the assignment operator (=).

Code: 5.12. Illustration of changing elements of a list.

```
#Illustration of changing elements to a list

datalist=[23, 45, 31, 53, 62]
datalist[2]=60
datalist[4]=12
print(datalist[:])
```

```
Output

[23, 45, 60, 53, 12]
```

An element can be added to a list by using the built-in Python method append() and if user wants to add more than one elements to a list then this can be performed with the help of Python built-in extend () method. The programming code for the same is given in Code: 5.13. In this program, we see that a new element 39 is added to the list by using the append () method. For adding more elements to a list extend () method is used, which adds three more elements to the datalist. Finally, the new updated list is displayed as shown in the output.

Code: 5.13. Illustration of adding elements to a list.

```
#Illustration of adding elements to a list

datalist=[23, 45, 31, 53, 62]
datalist.append(39)
datalist.extend([76, 23, 15])
print(datalist)
```

```
Output

[23, 45, 31, 53, 62, 39, 76, 23, 15]
```

5.2.4. List Methods

In the previous section, we discussed append() and extend () built-in methods of Python. Apart from that the Python language provides various built-in methods to make the use of list easier as compared to that of arrays in C, C++, or Java. The Table 5.5. presents various Python built-in methods to be applicable on lists with the description of each.

Method	Description
append(p)	Adds element p at the end of the list
extend(L)	Adds list L to the end of the existing list
insert(i, p)	Inserts element p at location i of the list

remove(p)	Removes first element, which is equal to p from the list
index(p)	Returns the index of first element that is equal to p
count(p)	Returns the occurrence (number of times) of element p in the list
pop([i])	Removes and returns item at location i in the list. (returns last item if i is not provided)
copy()	Returns a copy of the list
clear()	Removes all elements from the list and returns the empty list
sort()	Sorts the elements in the list
reverse()	Reverses the order of elements in the list

Table 5.5. Various Python list methods

All the methods provided in Table 5.5. are beneficial for implement data structures such as stack, queues, lists, etc. The programming example representing the use of above methods is given in Code 5.14. From the output of the program, the operation of each method can be understood very easily.

Note	All the list methods are accessed using dot (.) operator with the list name.

Code: 5.14. Illustration of list methods.

```
#Illustration of list methods


datalist=[23, 45, 31, 53, 62]
datalist.append(39)
datalist.extend([76, 23, 15])
print(datalist)
datalist.insert(2, 62)
print(datalist)
datalist.remove(23)
print(datalist)
print(datalist.index(53))
```

```
print(datalist.count(62))
datalist.pop()
print(datalist)
print(datalist.copy())
datalist.reverse()
print(datalist)
datalist.sort()
print(datalist)
print(datalist.clear())
```

Output

[23, 45, 31, 53, 62, 39, 76, 23, 15]
[23, 45, 62, 31, 53, 62, 39, 76, 23, 15]
[45, 62, 31, 53, 62, 39, 76, 23, 15]
3
2
[45, 62, 31, 53, 62, 39, 76, 23]
[45, 62, 31, 53, 62, 39, 76, 23]
[23, 76, 39, 62, 53, 31, 62, 45]
[23, 31, 39, 45, 53, 62, 62, 76]
None

5.2.5. List Functions

Function	Description
cmp(list1, list2)	Compares elements of both lists
len(list)	Gives the total length of the list
max(list)	Returns the largest element from the list
min(list)	Returns the smallest element from the list
list(seq)	Converts a tuple into list.

Table 5.6. List of Python built-in list functions

In addition to list methods as described in the previous section, the Python language also provides various list functions. The list of built-in Python list functions is given in Table 5.6. The programming illustration of len, max, and min is presented in Code 5.15. It is apparent from the output that the length of the given list is 5, the largest elements is 62 and the smallest element is 23.

Code: 5.15. Illustration of list functions.

```
#Illustration of list functions

datalist=[23, 45, 31, 53, 62]
print(len(datalist))
print(max(datalist))
print(min(datalist))
```

Output

```
5
62
23
```

5.2.6. List Comprehension

The Python language provides a very useful feature known as list comprehension. It provides an extremely efficient and concise way to create a new list from an existing one. In list comprehension, a for statement or an optional if statement is used to create a list from the wide range of list. All the process is performed inside square brackets representing a list. The programming illustration to extract even and odd numbers out of a list of 1 to 50 numbers is given in Code 5.16. In the programming code, we see that an even list is created out of list of 1 to 50 numbers based on the if condition i%2==0. Similarly, an odd list is created out of a list of 1 to 50 numbers based on the if condition i%2!=0. We can see from this feature that the Python language provides an efficient and concise codes for solving large problems. For instance in the programming Code 5.16., only one line of code is used to obtain even number from 1 to 50, that can be extended upto 1 to n numbers. The same is true for odd number list.

Code: 5.16. Illustration of list comprehension.

```
#Illustration of list comprehension

even=[i for i in range(50) if i%2 == 0]
print(even)
odd=[i for i in range(50) if i%2 != 0]
print(odd)
```

Output

[0, 2, 4, 6, 8, 10, 12, 14, 16, 18, 20, 22, 24, 26, 28, 30, 32, 34, 36, 38, 40, 42, 44, 46, 48]

[1, 3, 5, 7, 9, 11, 13, 15, 17, 19, 21, 23, 25, 27, 29, 31, 33, 35, 37, 39, 41, 43, 45, 47, 49]

5.2.7. List Membership Test

The most important data structure operation is the searching. In Python, an element from a list can be searched very easily. The 'in' operator is used to determine whether an element exists in the list. It returns true if elements exists otherwise false. The programming illustration for the same is given in Code 5.17. The code is quite simple. We search for the element 11 first, as it is present in the list so the output comes out to be true. The another test is performed for the element 66, as it does not exist in the list and thus the result is false.

Code:5.17. Illustration of list membership test.

```
#Illustration of list membership test


datalist=[11, 22, 33, 44, 55]
print( 11 in datalist)
print( 66 in datalist)
```

Output

True

> False

The 'in' operator is also used to iterate through the list using for loop. The programming example is presented in Code 5.18. It is apparent from the code that using for loop all the elements of the list can be accessed and processed efficiently.

Code: 5.18. Illustration of iterating through list.

```
#Illustration of iterating through list

for city in ['Goa', 'Mumbai', 'Chennai']:
        print("I visited", city)
```
Output
I visited Goa I visited Mumbai I visited Chennai

5.3. Python Tuples

In Python programming language, a tuple is another important data structure. A tuple is similar to Python list as studied in the previous section. The difference between tuple and list is that the elements in a list can be altered, whereas tuples are immutable, i.e., the elements of a tuple can not be changed.

5.3.1. Creating a Tuple

Alike list, it is very simple to create a tuple in Python. As we see earlier that the elements of a list are enclosed in square brackets [], whereas the elements of a tuple are enclosed in parenthesis () separated with commas. Moreover, a tuple can have any number of elements of heterogeneous type (integer, float, string, list, etc). The programming illustration to create different kinds of tuples is given in Code 5.19. In this program, we create three tuples. First tuple new_tuple is of homogeneous data elements. Second tuple new_tuple1 contains heterogeneous type data and the third tuple new_tuple2 represents the nested tuple, which also contains a list as its data element. The output for the same is given as well.

132

Code: 5.19. Illustration of creating a tuple.

```
#Illustration of creating a tuple

new_tuple=(1, 2, 3, 4)           # Homogeneous data elements
print(new_tuple)


new_tuple1=(1, "John", 55.5)    # Heterogeneous data elements
print(new_tuple1)


new_tuple2=[111, [1, "Clara", 75.5], (2, "Simon", 80.5)]#  Nested
tuple
print(new_tuple2)
```

```
Output

(1, 2, 3, 4)
(1, 'John', 55.5)
[111, [1, 'Clara', 75.5], (2, 'Simon', 80.5)]
```

5.3.2. Unpacking Tuple

The unpacking refers to separating members or elements of a tuple. Unpacking may be helpful for further processing tuple elements individually. The unpacking can be performed very easily as shown in Code 5.20. It is apparent from the output that the tuple elements can be separated for further use. In this program, the first element of the tuple is assigned to x, second element is assigned to y, and the third element is assigned to z. The programmer must take care while unpacking of tuple as the number of variables must match the number of elements of the tuple otherwise ValueError occurs.

Code: 5.20. Illustration of unpacking elements of a tuple.

```
#Illustration of unpacking a tuple
```

```
new_tuple2=(111, [1, "Clara", 75.5], (2, "Simon", 80.5))#  Nested
tuple
print(new_tuple2)

x, y, z=new_tuple2
print(x)
print(y)
print(z)
```

```
Output

111
[1, 'Clara', 75.5]
(2, 'Simon', 80.5)
```

5.3.3. Traversing Elements in a Tuple

As we have performed traversing of a list in the previous section, the similar concept is applicable over the tuple also. In the following sub sections we discuss the tuple traversing methods.

5.3.3.1. Indexing

Alike list the index of a tuple also starts from 0 and the index or subscript operator [] is used to access the elements of a tuple. If a tuple contains 10 elements then the index value of tuple varies from 0 to 9. Moreover, the index value must be an integer otherwise it will result into TypeError. The programming example to access elements of a tuple is presented in Code 5.21. In this program, a nested tuple is created with name datatuple, which contains 3 elements. We access 3 elements individually with index 0, 1, and 2. Then nested elements "Clara" and "Simon" are accessed by datatuple[1][1] and datatuple[2][1].

Code: 5.21. Illustration of traversing a tuple.

```
#Illustration of traversing a tuple

datatuple=(111, [1, "Clara", 75.5], (2, "Simon", 80.5))   #  Nested
                                                          #tuple
print(datatuple[0])
```

```
print(datatuple[1])
print(datatuple[2])
print(datatuple[1][1])
print(datatuple[2][1])
```

```
Output

111
[1, 'Clara', 75.5]
(2, 'Simon', 80.5)
Clara
Simon
```

5.3.3.2. Negative Indexing

As in Python list, negative indexing is also possible in tuple. The index -1 refers to the last element, -2 indexes the second last element, and so on. The programming illustration for the same is given in code 5.22. We can see from the program that the process of negative indexing is useful for traversing the tuple in reverse order.

Code: 5.22. Illustration of traversing a tuple by negative indexing.

```
#Illustration of traversing a tuple through negative indexing


datatuple=(111, [1, "Clara", 75.5], (2, "Simon", 80.5))        #  Nested
                                                               #tuple
print(datatuple[-1])
print(datatuple[-2])
print(datatuple[-3])
```

```
Output

(2, 'Simon', 80.5)
[1, 'Clara', 75.5]
111
```

5.3.3.3. Tuple Slicing

In order to access tuple elements for a certain range the slicing operator [:] is used. The programming example for using the slicing operator is given in Code 5.23. The slicing operator for tuple works the similar way as for list.

Code: 5.23. Illustration of slicing operator.

```
#Illustration of traversing a tuple by slicing operator

datatuple=('P', 'Y', 'T', 'H', 'O', 'N')
print(datatuple[1:3])
print(datatuple[-2:])
print(datatuple[:4])
```

```
Output

('Y', 'T')
('O', 'N')
('P', 'Y', 'T', 'H')
```

5.3.3.4. Changing/Updating a Tuple

As we know that tuples are immutable that means the elements of a tuple cannot be changed. However, if a tuple contains a list as its member then that member can be altered by using the index value of the list element. The programming example is given in Code 5.24. In this program, we see that only the list element at index value 1 can be altered. We change the value of "Clara" to "Sharon".

Code:5.24. Illustration of altering a tuple.

```
#Illustration of altering a tuple

new_tuple=(111, [1, "Clara", 75.5], (2, "Simon", 80.5))        # Nested
tuple
new_tuple[1][1]="Sharon"
print(new_tuple)
```

```
Output

(111, [1, 'Sharon', 75.5], (2, 'Simon', 80.5))
```

5.3.3.5. Deleting a Tuple

As mentioned in the previous section that the elements of a tuple cannot be altered. It implies that the elements of a tuple cannot deleted or removed. However, we can delete the entire tuple by using the del keyword. This concept is illustrated in Code 5.25. If user tries to print the deleted tuple then it will result into an error as shown in the output section.

Code 5.25. Illustration of deleting a tuple.

#Illustration of deleting a tuple datatuple=('P', 'Y', 'T', 'H', 'O', 'N') del datatuple print(datatuple)
Output 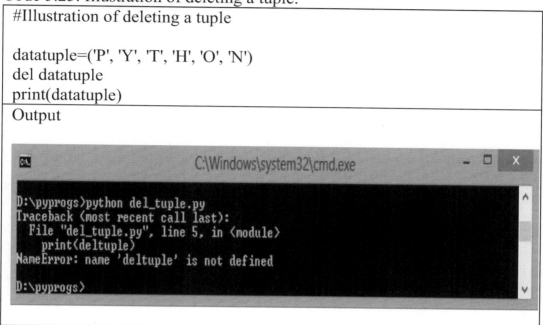

5.3.3.6. Python Tuple Methods

Since tuples are immutable, add and remove methods are not provided with tuples. The Python language contains only two methods for tuples, which are given in Table 5.6.

Method	Description
count(p)	It returns the number of times p occurs in the tuple
index(p)	It returns are index of first element in tuple, which is equal to p

Table 5.6. Python Tuple Methods

The programming illustration of the above methods is almost similar as that of list. Therefore, it is left as exercise for the reader. Apart from that the membership of an element of a tuple can be performed in the same way as that for list. The 'in' operator is used to determine the presence of an element in the tuple. If the element is present it returns true otherwise false. The 'in' operator can also be used for iterating through a tuple using for loop. The programming illustration is given in Code 5.26. In this code, it is apparent that all the elements of a tuple can be accessed efficiently using the in operator and for loop.

Code: 5.26. Illustration of accessing a tuple using for loop.

```
#Illustration of 'in' operator with tuple

for str in ('Bread', 'Butter', 'Jam'):
        print("I love", str)
```

```
Output

I love Bread
I love Butter
I love Jam
```

5.3.3.7. Python Tuple Functions

Apart from the tuple methods, the Python language also provides various tuple functions which are given in Table 5.7. with the description of each.

Function	Description
len()	Returns the total number of elements in the tuple
max()	Returns the largest element in the tuple
min()	Returns the smallest element in the tuple
sum()	Returns the sum of all the elements of the tuple
sort()	Returns the sorted list of elements of the tuple
enumerate()	Returns the enumerate object of the tuple
all()	Returns true if all the elements of the tuple are true
any()	Returns true if any element of the tuple is true

Table 5.7. Python tuple functions

5.3.3.8. Advantages of Tuple

Tuples are assumed to be similar to the lists with the major difference that tuples are immutable. Due to this feature, the tuple possesses certain advantages over Python list as given below:

1. The iteration over tuple is faster than list due to immutability of tuples.

2. In order to provide write protection to the data, tuples can be used.
3. Tuples containing immutable elements can be used as a key for a dictionary, which is not feasible with list.
4. Although list and tuple both can contain heterogeneous data elements. However, usually, tuples are used to contain heterogeneous data elements and lists are used to contain homogeneous data.

5.4. Python Sets

As we have learned in mathematics about sets, the Python language also provides a new data type called set to handle all set operations. A set is an unordered collection of elements. There is no duplicacy in the set and alike tuple, set is immutable (can not altered). A set can contain heterogeneous type of data. Since, set is an immutable data type, therefore, list or dicitonary can not be set members. As metioned earlier in Chapter 2, the sets can be used to perform all mathematical set operations such as union, intersection, difference, etc. In the following sub section, we will learn Python set in detail.

5.4.1. Creating a Set

A set is created by using the built-in Python function set(). All the elements of a set are placed inside the set function by enclosing within braces {} and separated by commas. The programming example to create a set in Python is given in Code 5.27.

In this program, we explore all the methods of creating a set in Python. In the first part, the set is created with name dataset1 by using the set() function. Secondly, a set is created without using the built-in set() function. The programmer must note that a set can also be created by putting its element into the curly braces. An empty set can also be created by leaving the curly braces {} empty as shown in the program. Then dataset4 contains heterogeneous kind of data, in which we see that the dataset4 contains 3 elements, where second element being a tuple. Consequently, the dataset5 is created with heterogeneous data set again. The dataset5 contains a list as its member. While executing this program, all the datasets from dataset1 through dataset4 provides the intended output. However, the printing of dataset5 results into an error, as list can not be a member of a set because Python sets are immutable entities and can not altered. Since, lists and dictionaries are mutable, they can not be a member of a set. The output can be seen in the output section of this program.

Code: 5.27. Illustration of creating a set in Python.

```python
# creating a set in Python

# creating a set by using set function
dataset1=set({1, 2, 3, 4})
print(dataset1)

# creating a set without using set function
dataset2={10, 20, 30, 40}
print(dataset2)

#creating an empty set
dataset3={}
print(dataset3)

#creating heterogeneous set with tuple as element
dataset4={1, (10, 20, 30), 5}
print(dataset4)

#creating heterogeneous set with list as element
dataset5={1, [10, 20, 30], 5}
print(dataset5)
```

Output

```
{1, 2, 3, 4}
{40, 10, 20, 30}
{}
{1, (10, 20, 30), 5}
```

```
D:\pyprogs>python python_set.py>output.txt
Traceback (most recent call last):
  File "python_set.py", line 20, in <module>
    dataset5={1, [10, 20, 30], 5}
TypeError: unhashable type: 'list'

D:\pyprogs>
```

5.4.2. Changing/Adding Elements to a Set

As it is mentioned earlier that, sets are immutable, i.e., we cannot change the value of any element of a set. Moreover, sets are unordered therefore, indexing has no meaning in context of sets. As a consequence of that we cannot access the elements of a set by specific indexing and slicing operator.

Nevertheless, an element can be added to a set by using the add() method. If user wishes to add more than one element, then this can be achieved by using the update() method of sets in Python. The programming illustration of using add() and update() methods is given in Code 5.28. In this program, we see that initially a dataset1 is created with 4 elements {10, 20, 30, 40}. Then, a new element 35 is added to the set by using add() method of Python sets. Subsequently, 3 more elements together are added to the dataset1 by using the update() method. It is to be noted that, more than one element can be added to the set using the update() method and in square brackets []. From the output of this program code, we see the intended results. Moreover, it is seen that the Python sets are unordered and the elements are displayed out of order despite of their actual assignment while creating the set. This demonstrates that indexing has no relevance in sets. Thus, slicing and indexing operators cannot be used with sets.

Code: 5.28. Illustration of updating Python set.

```
# updating a set in Python

dataset1={10, 20, 30, 40}
print(dataset1)
dataset1.add(35)
print(dataset1)

dataset1.update([5, 18, 27])
print(dataset1)
```
```
Output
{40, 10, 20, 30}
{40, 10, 35, 20, 30}
{35, 5, 40, 10, 18, 20, 27, 30}
```

5.4.3. Removing Elements from a Set

The Python language provides two methods discard() and remove() to remove elements from a set. Both of these functions perform the same task with only difference that if the element to be deleted does not exist in the set then remove() method raises an error. Whereas, the discard() method does not raise an error for the same case. The programming illustration for the same is given in Code 5.29. The program demonstrates that initially a dataset1 is created with 6 elements {10, 20, 30, 40, 50, 60}. Then, an element 30 is removed from the dataset by using the remove() method. Subsequently, an element 50 is deleted from the dataset1 using the discard() method. The updated dataset1 is printed after performing these two operations and we obtain the required output. Then, discard() method is used to remove 35 from the dataset1, although it does not exist in the set. It will not raise any error on the prompt. On the other hand, while using remove() method to eradicate 35 an error occurs as shown in the output section of this program.

Code: 5.29. Illustration of removing elements from a set.

```
# removing an element from a set

dataset1={10, 20, 30, 40, 50, 60}
print(dataset1)
dataset1.remove(30)
print(dataset1)

dataset1.discard(50)
print(dataset1)

dataset1.discard(35)
dataset1.remove(35)
```

Output
{40, 10, 50, 20, 60, 30}
{40, 10, 50, 20, 60}
{40, 10, 20, 60}

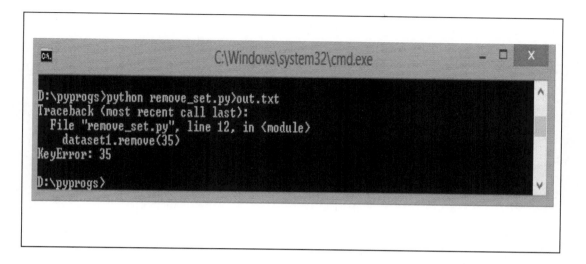

There exist another method pop() to remove an element from a Python set. Since, set is an unordered list of elements, the pop() method removes an element from the set randomly and user does not need to provide the value of a specific element to be deleted as that for remove() and discard() methods. The Python language provides another method clear() to remove all the elements of a set in one go. The programming illustration of pop() and clear() methods is given in Code 5.30. In this program, we see that by using the pop() method the element 40 has been removed from the set. The use of clear() method signifies the removal of all the elements of the set and an empty set is returned as an output.

Code: 5.30. Illustration of pop() and clear() methods.

```
#illustration of pop() and clear() methods

dataset={10, 20, 30, 40, 50, 60}
print(dataset)
dataset.pop()
print(dataset)

dataset.clear()
print(dataset)
```
Output

```
{40, 10, 50, 20, 60, 30}
{10, 50, 20, 60, 30}
set()
```

5.4.4. Python Set Operations

The basic set operations union, intersection, difference, and symmetric difference can be performed very efficiently over the Python sets. The description of each one of them is provided in the following sub sections.

5.4.4.1. Set Union

The union of elements of x and y is the set of all elements of both the sets. The duplicate elements are discarded in the union. The union of two sets x and y can be performed by using the operator (|) or by using the union() method. The programming illustration for the same is given in Code 5.31. It is apparent from the output that either by using the operator(|) or union() method, the result comes out to be the same.

Code: 5.31. Illustration of union of sets in Python.

```
#illustration of union operation on sets

x={10, 20, 30}
y={30, 40, 50, 60}

print(x|y)

print(x.union(y))
print(y.union(x))
```

```
Output

{50, 20, 40, 10, 60, 30}
{50, 20, 40, 10, 60, 30}
{50, 20, 40, 10, 60, 30}
```

5.4.4.2. Set Intersection

The intersection of sets x and y refers to the common elements of both the sets. The intersection of two sets can be performed either by using the (&) operator or the intersection() method of Python. The programming illustration for the intersection operation is given in Code 5.32. From the output section, we see that any of the three methods can be used to perform intersection of two sets. The result is the common elements {20, 30} of both the sets.

Code: 5.32. Illustration of intersection of sets in Python.

```
#illustration of intersection operation on set

x={10, 20, 30}
y={30, 20, 50, 60}

print(x&y)

print(x.intersection(y))
print(y.intersection(x))
```
```
Output
{20, 30}
{20, 30}
{20, 30}
```

5.4.4.3. Set Difference

The difference of two sets x and y, (x-y) results in elements of x but not in y. Likewise, (y-x) refers the elements of y but not in x. The intersection operation can be performed with the (-) operator or the difference() method of Python. The programming illustration of set difference is given in Code 5.33. It is apparent from the output that (x-y) and x.difference(y) results in elements of set x by excluding the elements of set y. Similarly, (y-x) and y.difference(x) results in elements of set y by excluding the elements of set x.

Code: 5.33. Illustration of difference of sets in Python.

```
#illustration of difference operation on set
```

```
x={10, 20, 30}
y={30, 40}

print(x-y)
print(x.difference(y))

print(y-x)
print(y.difference(x))
```

Output
{10, 20} {10, 20} {40} {40}

5.4.4.4. Set Symmetric Difference

The symmetric difference of sets x and y refers to a set of elements contained in both x and y except those which are common among them. The symmetric difference is performed using the (^) operator or by using the symmetric_difference() Python method. The programming illustration of this operation is given in Code 5.34. It is apparent from the output of this program that any of the four operations written in the code can be used to perform symmetric difference on two sets x and y.

Code: 5.34. Illustration of symmetric difference.

```
#illustration of symmetric difference operation on set

x={10, 20, 30}
y={30, 40}

print(x^y)
print(x.symmetric_difference(y))

print(y^x)
print(y.symmetric_difference(x))
```

```
Output

{40, 10, 20}
{40, 10, 20}
{40, 10, 20}
{40, 10, 20}
```

5.4.5. Python Set Methods

The python language offers various methods to be used in conjunction with sets. Many of them, we have discussed in the previous sub sections with their respective examples. The list of all the Python set methods is given in Table 5.8. with the description of each.

Method	Description
add()	Adds an element into a set
update()	Adds multiple elements into a set
discard()	Removes an element from the set. It does not raise error if element is not present in the set
remove()	Removes an element from the set. It raises error if element is not present in the set
pop()	Removes any random element from the set
clear()	Removes all the elements of the set
copy()	Returns a copy of the set
union()	Returns the union of two sets
intersection()	Returns common elements in two sets
difference()	Returns the difference of two sets
symmetric_difference()	Returns symmetric difference of two sets
difference_update()	Removes all elements of another set from this set
intersection_update()	Performs the intersection operation of this set and another set and updates the current set

symmetric_difference_update()	Updates the set with symmetric distance of itself and another.
issubset()	Returns true if another set contains this set
issuperset()	Returns true if this set contains another set
isdisjoint()	Returns true if two sets have null intersection. i.e., returns true if two sets contain no common elements

Table 5.8. List of Python set methods

5.4.6. The in Operator

As we have learned in the previous sections that 'in' operator is used to test the membership of a particular element in the list and tuple. Similarly, the 'in' operator can be used to determine the membership of a set element also. The programming illustration for the same is given in Code 5.35. It is apparent from this code that as 10 is the member of set x. Therefore, the result of 10 in x comes out to be true. However, the result of 50 in y is false as 50 is not a member of set y.

Code: 5.35. Illustration of membership test using 'in' operator.

```
#illustration of membership test of a set element

x={10, 20, 30}
y={30, 40}

print(10 in x)
print(50 in y)
```
```
Output

True
False
```

Alike lists and tuples the Python sets are also iterable. The 'in' operator is used with for loop to access all the elements of a set. The programming illustration for the same is given Code 5.36. This program illustrates that the set members can be accessed very efficiently by using for loop. The first set gx is created, which contains numeric values. Another set cities is created, which contains name of three cities. Subsequently, a third set is created with the set function, which contains a string "Kolkata". By using a for loop and in operator, all these three sets are accessed, which displays the elements of set in arbitrary order for all the three sets.

Code: 5.36. Illustration of accessing set elements using for loop.

```
#illustration of accessing set elements using for loop

gx={10, 20, 30, 40, 50}
cities={"Delhi", "Mumbai", "Goa"}

for n in gx:
        print(n)

for city in cities:
        print(city)

for c in set("Kolkata"):
        print(c)
```

Output

```
40
50
10
20
30
Goa
Mumbai
Delhi
a
t
l
o
K
k
```

5.4.7. Python Set Functions

The Python language offers a set of functions to be used with sets. All the Python set functions are listed in Table 5.9. All these functions are quite simple and can be programmed very easily.

Method	Description
all()	Returns true if all elements of the set are true
any()	Returns true if any element of the set is true. Returns false even if the set is empty
len()	Returns the total number of elements in the set
max()	Returns the largest element in the set
min()	Returns the smallest element in the set
sorted()	Returns a sorted list of elements of the set
sum()	Returns the sum of all the elements of the set
enumerate()	Returns an enumerate object

Table 5.9. List of Python set functions

5.4.8. Frozen Sets

The Python language offers a new datatype of sets called as frozenset. As indicated by the name, the elements of a frozen set cannot changed. As we know that tuples are immutable lists, similarly frozen sets are referred to as immutable sets. The frozenset() supports all the Python set methods except add(), remove() and discard() because the elements of frozensets can not be altered. The programming illustration of frozenset is given in Code 5.37. it is apparent from the code that yset is a normal set, therefore a new element 12 is added to it by using the add method. On the other hand, xset is a frozenset. therefore, adding an element to it raises an AttributeError as shown in the output section of this program.

Code: 5.37. Illustration of frozenset().

```
#illustration of frozenset()


yset={40, 50, 60}
yset.add(12)
print(yset)
```

```
xset=frozenset({10, 20, 30})
xset.add(12)
print(xset)
```

Output{40, 50, 60, 12}

```
C:\Windows\system32\cmd.exe                              _  □  X

D:\pyprogs>python frozen_set.py>out.txt
Traceback (most recent call last):
  File "frozen_set.py", line 9, in <module>
    xset.add(12)
AttributeError: 'frozenset' object has no attribute 'add'

D:\pyprogs>
```

5.5. Python Dictionary

In the previous sections, we learned sequence data types such as Python lists, tuples, and sets. Herein, this section, we learn Python dictionary. Python dictionary is a compound data type, which contains a pair comprising of a key value corresponding to value of an element. Or in other words, every data element of a dictionary is associated with a key value. The data element of a dictionary can be retrieved or accessed through its key value.

5.5.1. Creating a Dictionary

The Python dictionary is a collection of unordered pair of key values and its associated data elements. Dictionary contains heterogeneous kind of data, where key must be unique and of immutable type. In Python, a dictionary can be created as shown in Code 5.38. In this program, Python dictionary is created in four ways. The elements of a dictionary must be enclosed in curly braces {}. Initially data_dict1 is created containing two keys 'Name' and 'Rollno' with corresponding values. Then, a dictionary data_dict2 is created, which contains list as one its elements. Subsequently, data_dict3 is created using a Python built-in method dict(), which encloses the values of dictionary keys and their values. At last data_dict4 is created using dict() method, where keys and associated values are assigned as pairs. The output of all the 4 created dictionaries is given for more understanding.

Code: 5.38.Illustration of creating a Dictionary.

```
#Illustration of creating a dictionary in Python


data_dict1={'Name': 'Robin', 'Rollno': 111}
print(data_dict1)

data_dict2={'Name': 'Robin', 'Rollno': 111, 'Marks':[45, 67, 74] }
print(data_dict2)

data_dict3=dict({'Name': 'Sam', 'Rollno': 222})
print(data_dict3)

data_dict4=dict([('Name', 'Karl'), ('Rollno', 333)])
print(data_dict4)
```
```
Output


{'Name': 'Robin', 'Rollno': 111}
{'Name': 'Robin', 'Marks': [45, 67, 74], 'Rollno': 111}
{'Name': 'Sam', 'Rollno': 222}
{'Name': 'Karl', 'Rollno': 333}
```

5.5.2. Accessing a Dictionary

In the previous section, we learn how to create a dictionary in Python. We have also accessed the complete dictionary by printing the dictionary name using the Python built-in print() function. The method to access element values of a dictionary based on their key values is expressed in this section. The elements of a dictionary can be accessed in a very simple way. The programming illustration for the same is given in Code 5.39. In this program, we see that two dictionaries are created and their complete form is accessed using the print() function. However, the values of keys 'Name' and 'Rollno' are accessed using the square bracket [] referring the key term of the dictionary. In the program, the value of 'Name' and 'Rollno' are accessed using their respective keys. The Python language also provides a built-in method get() for fetching the value of a particular key of a dictionary. The output for the same can be seen in the output section of the given code.

Code: 5.39. Illustration of accessing a dictionary.

```
#Illustration of Accessing a Python Dictionary


data_dict1={'Name': 'Robin', 'Rollno': 111}
print(data_dict1)

data_dict2={'Name': 'Robin', 'Rollno': 111, 'Marks':[45, 67, 74] }
print(data_dict2)

print(data_dict1['Name'])
print(data_dict1['Rollno'])

print(data_dict2.get('Name'))
print(data_dict2.get('Rollno'))
print(data_dict2.get('Marks'))
```

Output

```
{'Rollno': 111, 'Name': 'Robin'}
{'Marks': [45, 67, 74], 'Rollno': 111, 'Name': 'Robin'}
Robin
111
Robin
111
[45, 67, 74]
```

5.5.3. Updating a Dictionary

The Python programmer can easily add or modify the elements of a dictionary. If the item is already present in the dictionary, then its value can be altered by providing new value to its key term. If the item does not exist in the dictionary, then a new key and its value can be added to the dictionary. The Code 5.40 illustrates this concept. In the program, we see that a dictionary data_dict is created with two keys values 'Name' and 'Rollno' with their values 'Robin' and 111 respectively. Now, we modify the value of key 'Rollno' to 222 and then add a new key value 'Marks' with its values as marks of three subjects provided as a list. Now, while printing the data_dict, we see that the updated values are displayed in output. Thus, we see that it is very simple to add or modify the elements of a Python dictionary.

Code: 5.40. Illustration of updating a Python dictionary.

```
#Illustration of updating a Python Dictionary


data_dict={'Name': 'Robin', 'Rollno': 111}
print(data_dict)

data_dict['Rollno']=222
data_dict['Marks']=[34, 28, 45]

print(data_dict)
```
```
Output

{'Name': 'Robin', 'Rollno': 111}
{'Name': 'Robin', 'Rollno': 222, 'Marks': [34, 28, 45]}
```

5.5.4. Removing or Deleting Elements of a Dictionary

The Python language provides two methods pop() and clear() to remove elements of a dictionary. The pop() method is used to remove the dictionary element with the specified key value. Another method popitem() can also be used to remove any element from the Python dictionary arbitrarily.

The clear() method is used to remove all the elements of a Python dictionary. Another method del is used to delete a specific element or entire dictionary. The programming illustration for same is given in Code 5.41. In this program, we see that a dictionary is created with four keys 'Name'. 'Rollno', 'Marks' and 'Mobile' with their corresponding values. Initially, pop() method is used to remove 'Rollno' from the dictionary. Then, popitem() is used to remove arbitrarily an element from the dictionary. In this program, 'Name' key with its value is removed. Next, del method is used to remove 'Mobile' key and value. At the end, the list is emptied by the clear method. The complete concept can be better understood by referring the output of the program.

Code: 5.41. Illustration of removing or deleting dictionary elements.

```
#Illustration of removing or deleting a Dictionary elements


data_dict={'Name': 'Robin', 'Rollno': 111, 'Marks':[40, 50, 60], 'Mobile':
9764377641}
print(data_dict)

print(data_dict.pop('Rollno'))
print(data_dict)

print(data_dict.popitem())

del data_dict['Mobile']
print(data_dict)

print(data_dict.clear())
```

Output

```
{'Rollno': 111, 'Name': 'Robin', 'Marks': [40, 50, 60], 'Mobile':
9764377641}
111
{'Name': 'Robin', 'Marks': [40, 50, 60], 'Mobile': 9764377641}
('Name', 'Robin')
{'Marks': [40, 50, 60]}
None
```

5.5.5. Python Dictionary Methods

The Python language provides various methods to be used with dictionaries. The list of dictionary methods is given in Table 5.10.

Method	Description
pop(key)	Removes an element from the dictionary whose key is given as its argument

popitem()	Removes an arbitrary element from the dictionary and returns its value
clear()	Removes all the elements of the dictionary
copy()	Creates a shallow copy of the dictionary
items()	Returns a new view of dictionary items
keys()	Returns a new view of dictionary keys
update([other])	Updates the dictionary with the specified key and value
get(key)	Returns the value of key

Table: 5.10. Python dictionary methods

5.5.6. Python Dictionary Membership Test

As studied earlier, the membership of a particular item in a list, tuple, or set is determined by using the 'in' operator. Similarly, 'in' operator is used with Python dictionary also to determine the presence of a particular key in the dictionary. It is to be noted here that the 'in' operator is applicable over dictionary keys and not on the values. It is demonstrated in Code 5.42. This program shows the use of 'in' operator. As the key 'Name' is present in the dictionary, therefore, the result of 'Name' in data_dict comes out to be True. Nevertheless, the values 'Robin' is tested by using the 'in' operator, which results in False, although 'Robin' is the member of data_dict. As mentioned earlier, the 'in' operator is applicable on keys only and not on values.

Code 5.42. Illustration of membership operator 'in'.

```
#Illustration of membership test of dictionary key

data_dict={'Name': 'Robin', 'Rollno': 111, 'Marks':[40, 50, 60]}

print('Name' in data_dict)
print('Robin' in data_dict)
```
Output

True
False

Alike, list and tuple, the Python dictionaries are iterable. The elements of Python dictionary can be accessed through for loop as shown in Code: 5.43. It can be seen from the program that the individual element values of the dictionary are accessed using for loop. If the programmer uses the statement print(i) only inside the for loop, then dictionary keys will be iterated.

Code: 5.43. Illustration of dictionary iteration using for loop.

```
#Illustration of using for loop with dictionary

data_dict={'Name': 'Robin', 'Rollno': 111, 'Marks':[40, 50, 60]}


for i in data_dict:
        print(data_dict[i])
```
Output
Robin 111 [40, 50, 60]

5.5.7. Python Dictionary Functions

The Python language provides built-in functions to be used with dictionary. The list is tabulated in Table 5.11.

Function	Description
sorted()	Sorts the elements of dictionary
len()	Returns the length of the dictionary
cmp()	Compares items of two dictionaries
any()	Returns true if any of the dictionary item is true
all()	Returns true if all the items of the dictionary are true

Table: 5.11. Python Dictionary Functions

5.6. Python Strings

The collection or sequence of characters is called a string. As Python list contain a sequence of heterogeneous data elements, the string contains a contiguous sequence of characters, which can be alphabets or special characters. We know that computer understands only binary data either 0 or 1. All the data that we type and use in the computer is first converted into binary form. Therefore, the strings that is alphabetical or character data is also converted into equivalent binary code using some encoding technique such as ASCII or Unicode encoding. In Python, Unicode encoding is used for strings. The Unicode encoding is used to bring uniformity as it includes all the characters of all the languages. String is a useful data element of Python as it is used to store character values such as name, city, class, etc.

5.6.1. Creating a String in Python

The creation of string is rather simple in Python. The programmer does not need to specify the string size as in C, C++, and Java. The programmer can create a string of any size. The programming illustration of creating a string is given in Code 5.44. In this program, three strings are created with name new_string1, new_string2, and new_string3. In the first string, the value 'Python' is assigned in single quotes. In the second string, the value "Python" is assigned in double quotes and in the last one triple quotes are used to assign the value. Thus, a string value can be provided in either in single, double, or triple quotes.

Code: 5.44. Illustration of creating a string.

#Illustration of creating a string new_string='Python' print(new_string) new_string1="Python" print(new_string1) new_string2="""Python""" print(new_string2)
Output Python Python

Python

5.6.2. Accessing String Characters

Since string is a sequence of characters, then string characters can be accessed by using the index operator or the slicing operator. The similar method is used that we have performed for lists and tuples. The programming illustration for the same is given in Code 5.45. In the program, it is clear that the particular character of a string can be accessed by specifying its index. The indexing starts from 0. The negative indexing is also possible, which is used to access elements from the end of the string. In the example, the slicing operator [:] is also used to print the string characters upto certain range by excluding the last specified index value. The last character of string represented by -1 indicates 'n' in Python string. -2 indicates 'o', -3 represents 'h', and so on.

Code: 5.45. Illustration of accessing string characters.

```
#Illustration of accessing a string

new_string='Python'
print(new_string[0])
print(new_string[3])
print(new_string[-1])
print(new_string[1:3])
print(new_string[:-2])
```

Output

```
P
h
n
yt
Pyth
```

5.6.3. Changing or Deleting String Characters

Similar to tuple, the string characters are also immutable. That means we cannot change or add elements to an existing string. However, the complete string can be deleted by using the del keyword. The programming illustration for the same is given in Code 5.46. In this example, we see that changing the character at index location [3] raise an error 'str' object does not support item assignment. Then print(new_string) statement also raises an error as del new_string has deleted the string and new_string does not exist.

Code: 5.46. Illustration of deleting a string.

```
#Illustration of changing/deleting a string

new_string='Python'

new_string[3]='k'
del new_string
print(new_string)
```

Output

5.6.4. Python String Operations

5.6.4.1. Concatenation

The concatenation operation is used for adding two strings. This can be achieved by using the '+' operator between two strings. In Python the '*' operator can also be used to repeat a particular string a specified number of times. The demonstration of both '+' and '*' operator is given in Code 5.47. As described, the '+' operator has concatenated two strings string1 and string 2 and the '*' operator has repeated the string1 three times. The output can be referred for more clarity of the concept.

Code: 5.47. Illustration of using '+' and '*' operators with string.

```
#Illustration of using '+' and '*' operators with string


string1='Hello'
string2=' Welcome to Python Programming'

print(string1+string2)

print(string1 * 3)
```

```
Output

Hello Welcome to Python Programming

HelloHelloHello
```

5.6.4.2. Iteration and Membership Test

Since string is a sequence of characters, the string can be iterated by using for loop as shown in Code 5.48. In this program a string is created with value 'Python Programming'. The values of all the string characters are accessed by using for loop. As performed for list, tuple, and set, in the previous sections, the presence of a string member can be determined using 'in' operator. This is also illustrated in the programming code, which results in false for 'p' membership test. This is because the string1 contains capital letter 'P' and not the small one. Subsequently, the test for character 't' comes out to be true.

Code: 5.48. Accessing string characters using for loop.

```
#Illustration of using for loop with string

string1='Python Programming'
for i in string1:
        print (i)

print('p' in string1)
print('t' in string1)
```

Output

```
P
y
t
h
o
n

P
r
o
g
r
a
m
m
i
n
g
False
True
```

5.6.5. String Formatting

A string can be formatted by using escape sequences and format symbols. The escape sequences are non printable characters which provide good display for the output. These are used with back slash. The Python string escape sequences are listed in Table 5.12.

Escape Sequence	Description
\\	Backslash
\'	Single quote
\"	Double quote
\b	ASCII Backspace
\a	ASCII Bell
\f	ASCII Formfeed
\n	ASCII Linefeed
\r	ASCII Carriage Return
\t	ASCII Horizontal Tab
\v	ASCII Vertical Tab
\ooo	Character with octal value ooo
\xHH	Character with hexadecimal value HH

Table 5.12. List of escape sequences

The format symbols are already explained in Chapter 2 under Section 2.10.2.

5.6.6. Python String Built-in Methods

The Python language provides a list of methods to manipulate strings. The methods are listed in Table 5.13. These string methods are very easy to use by using the dot operator with the string name. For example the string length is determined as print(string1.len()). This statement prints the length of the string, i.e., total number of characters of the string1.

Method	Description
len(string)	Returns the length of the string
max(str)	Returns the max alphabetical character from the string str.

min(str)	Returns the min alphabetical character from the string str.
upper()	Converts lowercase letters in string to uppercase.
lower()	Converts all uppercase letters in string to lowercase.
capitalize()	Capitalizes first letter of string
center(width, fillchar)	Returns a space-padded string with the original string centered to a total of width columns.
isdigit()	Returns true if string contains only digits and false otherwise.
isalpha()	Returns true if string has at least one character and all characters are alphabetic and false otherwise.
isalnum()	Returns true if string has at least one character and all characters are alphanumeric and false otherwise.
islower()	Returns true if string has at least one cased character and all cased characters are in lowercase and false otherwise.
isupper()	Returns true if string has at least one cased character and all cased characters are in uppercase and false otherwise.
count(str, beg= 0,end=len(string))	Counts how many times str occurs in string or in a substring of string if starting index beg and ending index end are given.
index(str, beg=0, end=len(string))	Same as find(), but raises an exception if str not found.
istitle()	Returns true if string is properly "titlecased" and false otherwise.
isnumeric()	Returns true if a unicode string contains only numeric characters and false otherwise.
swapcase()	Inverts case for all letters in string.
title()	Returns "titlecased" version of string, that is, all words begin with uppercase and the rest are lowercase.
isdecimal()	Returns true if a unicode string contains only decimal characters and false otherwise.
isspace()	Returns true if string contains only whitespace characters and false otherwise.

Table 5.13. List of Python String Methods

5.7. Summary

In this chapter, we learned the Python native data types thoroughly. The Python language contains number, string, list, tuple, set, and dictionary, data types. These are the different ways to store data in Python. The number and string data types store numeric and character data respectively. Whereas, list, tuple, set, and dictionary store heterogeneous data sequentially. However, set and dictionary represent unordered representation of data. All the methods and functions associated with these data types are described with the programming illustration of each.

Review Questions

Q.1 What do you understand by data types in Python language? Name different data types available in Python.

Q.2 How would you save a numeric data in Python? Illustrate with a programming example.

Q.3 How type conversion is performed in numbers? Write down all the type conversion functions.

Q.4 List all the mathematical functions to be used in Python with the description of each.

Q.5 List trigonometric functions available in Python.

Q.6 What are random numbers? How random numbers are used in Python?

Q.7 Describe Python mathematical constants.

Q.8 What are Python lists? How would you create a list in Python? Explain with a suitable programming example.

Q.9 Describe various ways to traverse a list in Python.

Q.10 What do you understand by negative indexing in Python?

Q.11 What is the significance of slicing?

Q.12 List all the Python list methods.

Q.13 Describe all the Python list functions.

Q.14 How list comprehension is performed in Python? Explain with suitable example.

Q.15 What do you understand by Python tuples? How would you create a tuple?

Q.16 What do you understand by unpacking tuples?

Q.17 Describe various ways to traverse a tuple in Python.

Q.18 How a tuple or a list can be deleted in Python?

Q.19 List all tuple methods with the description of each.

Q.20 List all tuple functions with the description of each.

Q.21 What are Python sets? How would you create them? Explain.

Q.22 How update, change, remove operations are performed on Python tuples?

Q.23 Discuss various set operations with the programming demonstration of each.

Q.24 What are frozen sets? Elaborate.

Q.25 List all Python set methods and functions with the purpose of each.

Q.26 What do you understand by Python dictionary? How would you create a dictionary?

Q.27 Elaborate the ways to access a dictionary in Python?

Q.28 What does a key refers to in a dictionary in Python?

Q.29 How update, removal, and changing of elements of dictionary is performed Python?

Q.30 Describe all the Python dictionary methods and functions with purpose of each of them.

Q.31 What are strings in Python? How would you create a string?

Q.32 How can the characters of a string be accessed?

Q.33 How would you perform deletion and updation of a string in Python?

Q.34 How concatenation and repetition is performed in Python strings?

Q.35 What are various string formatting methods? Explain.

Q.36 Describe all the Python string built-in methods.

Q.37 How for loop is used to access list, tuple, set, string, and dictionary in Python? Elaborate with a programming example.

Programming Exercises

1. Write a program to compute sum of first n natural numbers.
2. Write a program to compute factorial of number within a specific range. For example from 35 to 75.
3. Write a program to determine prime numbers within a specific range.
4. Write a program to count the number of persons of age above 60 and below 90.
5. Write a program to compute transpose of a matrix.
6. Write a program to add two matrices.

7. Write a program to subtract two matrices.
8. Write a program to multiply two matrices.
9. Write a program to display a multiplication table.
10. Write a program to count the occurrence of each vowel.
11. Write a program compute the total number of vowels in a word.
12. Write a program to determine whether a string is palindrome or not.
13. Write a program to insert an element into a list.
14. Write a program to delete an element from a list.
15. Write a program to delete an entire list.
16. Write a program to sort a list of numbers.
17. Write a program to sort words in alphabetical order.
18. Write programs to illustrate all the set operations in Python.
19. Write a program to maintain books as per their serial number in library using dictionary.
20. Write a program to insert, delete, and change elements of a dictionary in Python.

CHAPTER 6

Python Functions

Highlights

- Python functions
- Types of functions
- Advantages of functions
- Python user defined functions
- Python anonymous functions
- Pass by value vs. pass by reference
- Recursion

In programming, sometimes a similar code has to be repeated at many places in a program. For which, the programmer needs to write the same set of instructions several times. For example, while computing a binomial coefficient, the factorial needs to be computed several times. It would waste the programmer's time and effort to write the same code again and again. This activity not only increases the size of the program but also leads to typographical errors. To overcome this issue, the Python programming language is provided with the feature called subprograms or functions. A subprogram or function is a name given to a set of instructions that can be called by another program or a subprogram. This technique simplifies the programming process to a great extent because a single set of instructions in the form of a subprogram is being used for all instances of computational requirements with only change in the supplied data.

6.1. Python Functions

In Python programming language, a function is a self-contained group of statements, which are intended to perform a specific task. Functions break the program into smaller modules, which perform a particular operation and are easy to understand. The large programs become more manageable and organized by using the concept of functions.

6.2. Advantages of Functions

1. **Avoids Repetition:** functions avoid repetition of the similar code again and again. The same code of a function can be used several times by different parts of the program or by different programs.
2. **Modularization:** decomposing a large program into smaller modules makes the designing of the program faster and easier. Different programmers can work on different modules, which can be further combined to make the larger complete program.
3. **Reduce Size:** the size of the source program can be reduced considerably by using functions appropriately in the program.
4. **Logical Precision:** the use of user defined functions allows a large program to be broken into smaller self-contained blocks or components, which is intended to perform a specific and unique function. By the use of functions, the program becomes easier to code and debug.
5. **Save Memory Requirement:** different set of data can be transferred to the function each time when it is called. The use of

functions saves huge memory space by allowing same set of statements to be used for different set of data.

6. **Portable:** functions can be used in many programs, which encourages portability.

6.3. Types of Functions

Alike C/C++/Java, Python functions can be divided into the following two types:

1. Built-in functions - Functions that are built into Python.
2. User-defined functions - Functions defined by the users themselves.

6.4. Built-in Functions

The functions are already provided by the Python are called built-in functions. The programmer can use built-in functions readily without any additional effort to code that function. The functions, which we have already used in previous chapters such as print(), abs(), random(), range(), print(), input(), eval(), etc. In Python version 3.5.1. 68 built-in functions are available (which may vary depending on the different versions). The built-in functions are listed in Table 6.1., with the description of each.

Built-in Function	Description
abs()	Returns the absolute value of a number.
all()	Returns True if all elements of the iterable are true (or if the iterable is empty).
any()	Returns True if any element of the iterable is true. If the iterable is empty, return False.
ascii()	Returns a string containing a printable representation of an object, but escape the non-ASCII characters.
bin()	Converts an integer number to a binary string.

bool()	Converts a value to a Boolean.
bytearray()	Returns a new array of bytes.
bytes()	Returns a new "bytes" object.
callable()	Returns True if the object argument appears callable, False if not.
chr()	Returns the string representing a character.
classmethod()	Returns a class method for the function.
compile()	Compiles the source into a code or AST object.
complex()	Creates a complex number or convert a string or number to a complex number.
delattr()	Deletes the named attribute of an object.
dict()	Creates a new dictionary.
dir()	Returns the list of names in the current local scope.
divmod()	Returns a pair of numbers consisting of quotient and remainder when using integer division.
enumerate()	Returns an enumerate object.
eval()	The argument is parsed and evaluated as a Python expression.
exec()	Dynamic execution of Python code.
filter()	Constructs an iterator from elements of iterable for which function returns true.
float()	Converts a string or a number to floating point.
format()	Converts a value to a "formatted" representation.
frozenset()	Returns a new frozenset object.
getattr()	Returns the value of the named attribute of an object.
globals()	Returns a dictionary representing the current global symbol table.
hasattr()	Returns True if the name is one of the object's attributes.
hash()	Returns the hash value of the object.
help()	Invokes the built-in help system.
hex()	Converts an integer number to a hexadecimal string.
id()	Returns the "identity" of an object.
input()	Reads a line from input, converts it to a string (stripping a trailing newline), and returns that.
int()	Converts a number or string to an integer.

isinstance()	Returns True if the object argument is an instance.
issubclass()	Returns True if class is a subclass.
iter()	Returns an iterator object.
len()	Returns the length (the number of items) of an object.
list()	Returns a list.
locals()	Updates and return a dictionary representing the current local symbol table.
map()	Returns an iterator that applies function to every item of iterable, yielding the results.
max()	Returns the largest item in an iterable.
memoryview()	Returns a "memory view" object created from the given argument.
min()	Returns the smallest item in an iterable.
next()	Retrieves the next item from the iterator.
object()	Returns a new featureless object.
oct()	Converts an integer number to an octal string.
open()	Opens file and returns a corresponding file object.
ord()	Returns an integer representing the Unicode.
pow()	Returns power raised to a number.
print()	Prints objects to the stream.
property()	Returns a property attribute.
range()	Returns an iterable sequence.
repr()	Returns a string containing a printable representation of an object.
reversed()	Returns a reverse iterator.
round()	Returns the rounded floating point value.
set()	Returns a new set object.
setattr()	Assigns the value to the attribute.
slice()	Returns a slice object.
sorted()	Returns a new sorted list.
staticmethod()	Returns a static method for function.
str()	Returns a str version of object.
sum()	Sums the items of an iterable from left to right and returns the total.
super()	Returns a proxy object that delegates method calls to a parent or sibling class.

tuple()	Returns a tuple
type()	Returns the type of an object.
vars()	Returns the __dict__ attribute for a module, class, instance, or any other object.
zip()	Makes an iterator that aggregates elements from each of the iterables.
import__()	This function is invoked by the import statement.

Table 6.1. Python built-in functions.

Before calling any of the built-in functions the appropriate module must be imported first in the Python script by using the import command, otherwise the module does not get executed. For example for using mathematical functions such as pow(), sqrt(), abs(), math module is required to be imported beforehand the program code.

6.5. Python User Defined Functions

As we have seen in the previous section that Python contains a rich set of built-in functions. However, the programmer can develop their own functions depending upon their requirement and such functions are termed as user defined functions. In formal language, functions that are defined by us to perform certain specific operation or task are termed as user-defined functions.

Formally, the user defined functions contain two parts:

- Function Definition: contains the actual code for the operation to be performed.
- Function Call: where the call to the function definition is made to perform a specific operation.

6.5.1. Function Definition (Defining a Function in Python)

Unlike C/C++/Java, the format of Python user defined functions is different. The syntax of user defined functions is given below:

```
def function_name(list of parameters):
```

```
        "docstring"
        statement(s)
        return(parameter)
```

The above syntax of function definition has the following components:

1. The keyword def symbolizes the start of the function header.
2. A function name to uniquely identify it. Function naming follows the similar rules that are used for writing identifiers as described in Chapter 2.
3. List of parameters also called as list of arguments through which value is passed to the function. The list of parameters is optional.
4. A colon (:) to mark the end of function header.
5. Optional documentation string (docstring) is used to describe purpose of the function, which is slightly similar to python documentation using comment.
6. Python statements that perform the intended task for which the user defined function is made. It is mandatory to maintain the indentation level while writing python statements in the function definition.
7. At the end an optional return statement is used to return a value (result) from the function. This statement can contain an optional parameter to return the computed result back to the function call. If there is no parameter in the statement or the return statement is not mentioned at the end of function definition then function returns the None object.

6.5.2. Function Call

The function definition described above provides the code that is intended to perform a certain operation based on parameters given and statements written. Once the function definition is finalized, the programmer can call it from other function or from the Python prompt. This can be done by just writing the function name and specifying the list of parameters (if desired). Consider the following program Code 6.1. which, prints a message using Python user defined function.

Code: 6.1. Illustration of Python user defined function.

```
# This program illustrates the Python user defined function

#function definition of print_msg()
def print_msg(str):
        "This function prints the value of str passed as a
paremeter"
        print(str)
        return

# function call of print_msg()
print_msg("print_msg is a user defined function.")
print_msg("another call to print_msg function.")
print_msg("Hello, Welcome to Python Programming!")
```

Output

```
print_msg is a user defined function.
another call to print_msg function.
Hello, Welcome to Python Programming!
```

6.5.3. Types of Function Arguments (Parameters)

In Python user defined functions can be used with different types of argument lists. The types are given as follows:

1. Functions with no arguments
2. Functions with required arguments
3. Functions with variable arguments
4. Functions with keyword based arguments
5. Functions with default arguments

6.5.3.1. Functions with No Arguments

Alike, C and C++, Python user defined functions can be defined without specifying argument list. Such functions perform the intended task on its own without fetching any data from the function call. The programming code representing function with no argument is displayed in Code 6.2. In the program we see that the function print_msg() prints the message without fetching it as an argument from the function call. Another example to compute sum of two numbers without any argument passing is given in Code 6.3. We can see that the program very effectively produces the output and displays the result as desired.

Code: 6.2. Illustration of function with no argument list.

```
# This program illustrates the Python user defined function with
no argument list

def print_msg():
        "This function prints the message"
        print('Hello, Welcome to Python Programming!')
        return


# function call of print_msg()
print_msg()
```

Output
Hello, Welcome to Python Programming!

Code: 6.3. Illustration of function to compute sum of two numbers without argument list.

```
# This program illustrates the Python user defined function with
no argument list

def sum():
        "This function computes sum of two numbers"
        a=10
        b=20
        print('sum={0}'.format(a+b))
        return

# function call of print_msg()
sum()
```

Output
Sum=30

6.5.3.2. Functions with Required Arguments

While making a function call, a list of arguments is supplied, which is fetched by the function definition. The arguments passed must be in correct positional order and must match exactly with that of function definition. The program signifying the use of required arguments is given in Code: 6.4. The program computes the sum of two numbers by using functions with required arguments. We see that two values 10 and 20 are passed as arguments to function sum(), which then produces the intended output. Another example of the same program with using return statement is given in Code 6.5. We see that the computed result is sent back to the calling function by the return statement and the result is displayed after the function call and not in the function definition.

Code: 6.4. Illustration of function to compute sum of two numbers with required argument list.

```
# This program illustrates the Python user defined function with
argument list

def sum(a, b):
        "This function computes sum of two numbers"
        print('sum={0}'.format(a+b))
        return



# function call of print_msg()
sum(10, 20)
```

Output
Sum=30

Code: 6.5. Illustration of function to compute sum of two numbers with required argument list and return statement.

```
# This program illustrates the Python user defined function with
argument list and return statement

def sum(a, b):
        "This function computes sum of two numbers"
        return (a+b)


# function call of print_msg()
s=sum(10, 20)
print('sum={0}'.format(s))
```
Output

Sum=30

If the user does not supply the argument value, where argument is desired then the Python interpreter generates an error message. This is illustrated in the Code: 6.6. and the output is given in Fig. 6.1.

Code: 6.6. Illustration of not specifying required argument list.

```
# This program illustrates the Python user defined function with
no required argument list

def sum(a, b):
        "This function computes sum of two numbers"
        print('sum={0}'.format(a+b))
        return


# function call of print_msg()
sum()
```

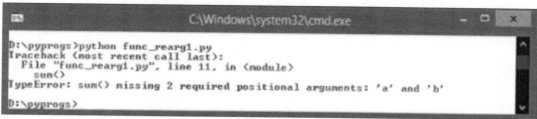

Fig. 6.1. Output of Code 6.6.

6.5.3.3. Functions with Arbitrary Length Arguments

In the above, we have discussed functions without list of arguments and with list of required arguments. The Python language has the feature of variable length arguments in which programmer can specify any number of arguments depending upon the requirement. The syntax of arbitrary length arguments is as under:

```
def function_name(*var_args_tuple):
        "function documentation using Docstring"
        statement(s)
        return(expression)
```

An asterisk (*) preceding the variable name is intended to hold the values of all non keyword arbitrary arguments. This tuple remains empty if no additional arguments are specified during the function call. The programming code illustrating the concept of variable length arguments is given in Code: 6.7. In this program, a variable list is passed as an argument to the var_func() with values from 10, 20, ..., 100. The concept of arbitrary length arguments is used for passing tuple or lists as arguments. It is similar to passing array elements to a function in C. However, in Python the method to perform the same is rather simple.

Code: 6.7. Illustration of variable length arguments passed to a user defined function.

```
# This program illustrates the Python user defined function with
arbitrary length arguments

def var_func(*list):
        "This function prints variable passed as arguments"
        for i in list:
                print(i)
        return



# function call of print_msg()
var_func(10, 20, 30, 40, 50, 60, 70, 80, 90, 100)
```

```
Output:

10
20
30
40
50
60
70
80
90
100
```

6.5.3.4. Functions with Keyword Based Arguments

In keyword based arguments, a value is assigned to the argument in the function call. While passing keyword based arguments, the caller identifies the arguments by parameter name. By using this feature, the programmer can place arguments out of order. As, it is the responsibility of the interpreter to use the keywords to match the values with parameters. The programming in Code 6.8. represents the concept of keyword based arguments. It is apparent from the output that in the function call the argument Name is passed first and empID is passed at second place. However, the function definition receives the parameter values based on the keywords supplied rather than the order in which they are passed.

Code: 6.8. Illustration of variable length arguments passed to a user defined function.

```
# This program illustrates the Python user defined function with
keyword based arguments

def employee_info(empID, Name):
        print(empID)
        print(Name)
        return


# function call of print_msg()
employee_info(Name="John", empID=1234)
```

Output:

```
1234
John
```

6.5.3.5. Functions with Default Arguments

A default argument is used to set default value of an argument for which a value is not passed by the function call. Then that default value is fetched by the function definition for further computations. The program representing the concept of default value argument is given in Code 6.9. It can be seen that in the first call to function employee_info(), all the arguments are passed with a value. However, in the second call to employee_info() only the value of argument empID is passed and rest two default values of Name and salary are taken up by the function definition.

Code: 6.9. Illustration of default arguments passed to a user defined function.

```
# This program illustrates the Python user defined function with
default arguments


def employee_info(empID, Name='John', salary=8000):
        print(empID)
        print(Name)
        print(salary)
        return



# function call of print_msg()
employee_info(Name="Harry", empID=1111, salary=10000)
employee_info(empID=2222)
```

```
Output:

1111
Harry
10000
2222
John
8000
```

6.6. Python Anonymous Functions

Python supports the development of an additional type of function definition known as anonymous function. These functions are termed as anonymous because they do not follow the standard method by using the *def* keyword and anonymous functions are not bound to a name. These are created at runtime, using the construct known as *lambda*. The syntax of lambda is as follows:

```
lambda arg1, arg2, ..., argn: expression
```

6.6.1. Characteristics of Lambda Form (Anonymous Function)

- lambda form can take multiple arguments as shown in the syntax and returns only one value computed through the expression.
- It does not contain multiple line of statement block as in standard Python functions.
- Since, an expression is required in lambda form, direct call to print() function can not be made in lambda form of anonymous function.
- As no additional statements can be written in lambda form, it has only local namespace that means it can use only those variables that are passed as arguments to it or which are in the global scope.
- The lambda form (anonymous functions) can not be considered as C/C++ inline functions, as they contain only single line of statement. The concept of Python anonymous function is entirely different from the C/C++ inline function and can be used with typical functional concepts.

The programming example illustrating the use of lambda function is given in Code: 6.10. This program computes the product of two numbers, by using anonymous function. We see that the variable product is used as a function name while calling and passing the argument values to the lambda (anonymous function). Lambda is just a single line statement, which performs the intended task and the result is assigned to product variable. The function print() prints the value of the computed product using lambda function. The similar program to compute product of two numbers without using lambda anonymous function is presented in Code: 6.11.

Code: 6.10. Illustration of anonymous functions (lambda form).

```
# This program illustrates the concept of lambda form (anonymous
function)

#anonymous function definition
product=lambda a, b:a*b


#product can be called as function as follows
print('Product={0}'.format(product(12, 10)))
print('Product={0}'.format(product(50, 10)))
```

Output

```
Product=120
Product=500
```

Code: 6.11. Illustration of computation of product without using anonymous functions.

```
# This program illustrates the Product of two numbers

def product(a, b):
        "This function computes product of two numbers"
        print('product={0}'.format(a*b))
        return


# function call of product()
product(10, 20)
```

Output

```
Product=200
```

6.7. Pass by Value vs. Pass by Reference

As we know that the two way communication between function caller and function definition is achieved through arguments, which we pass by function call. In Python language arguments can be passed by value and by object reference.

6.7.1. Pass by Value

This concept can be understood by considering the program for passing arguments by value in Code: 6.12. It is perceived from the output of the program that a list object is created with values 1, 2, 3 and it is passed as an argument to the function update(). In the function definition of update, we see that the list values are modified to 100, 200, 300 and the result is printed, which displays the new values. However, when the function update() returns back and the value of list is printed out to be the old ones, i.e., 1, 2, 3 and not the updated ones. This concept is known as pass by value, which signifies that if any modifications are made to the values in the function definition then it does not make any effect on the arguments of the caller function.

Code: 6.12. Illustration of call by value.

```
# This program demonstrates the concept of call by value

#function definition
def update(list):
        'This function updates the passed values'
        list=[100, 200, 300]
        print('inside function', list)
        return

# Function call of update() function
list=[1, 2, 3]
update(list)
print('after returning from function', list)
```
Output

inside function [100, 200, 300]

after returning from function [1, 2, 3]

6.7.2. Pass by Object Reference

A program representing the concept of pass by object reference is given in Code: 6.13. We can see from this program that unlike the call by value, where the list values were modified in the function definition of Code: 6.12, here in Code 6.13., the list function append is used to add more items in the list. From the output, it is observed that the new values are appended after the old ones and the similar result is printed both in function definition and after the function call.

Code: 6.13. Illustration of call by reference.

```
# This program demonstrates the concept of call by reference

#function definition
def update(list):
        'This changes a passed into this function'
        list.append([100, 200, 300])
        print('inside function', list)
        return

# Function call of update() function
list=[1, 2, 3]
update(list)
print('after returning from function', list)
```
Output

```
inside function [1, 2, 3, [100, 200, 300]]
after returning from function [1, 2, 3, [100, 200, 300]]
```

After, observing the results of both call by value and call by reference, it is perceived that in Python language, the arguments are passed by object reference intrinsically. Any change, made to the arguments in the function definition does not affect the object on the function call side. However, if any in-build function such as append() is associated with the function argument in the function definition, then it definitely make changes to the object and the object value gets updated on both function definition as well as function call side.

6.8. Recursion

Alike C/C++, a function can call itself, rather than from any other function. This concept is termed as recursion. Recursive functions act like loops that they iterate within the function to perform some operation. The programmer must consider some points while using recursion, which are

- Recursion can be used for any function involving loops.
- While developing programs using recursion, the programmer must follow some guidelines, such as
    - There must be a key variable, which will be responsible for the termination of recursion.
    - To determine the base value, which the key variable has to meet to reach the termination.
    - To make sure the key variable must approach the base value in every recursive call.
    - To make the recursive function terminate when the key variable reaches the base value.

The programming example to compute factorial of a given number using recursion is presented in Code: 6.14. In this program, initially the function call fact(num) is made with the number input by the user. In the function definition, recursive calls are made to function fact() with the value of n is decrementing by 1 in every recursive call. This process continues until the value of n becomes 1. Then, the function fact() computes the factorial by returning the values recursively. The Fig.6.2. displays the computation of recursive factorial function.

Code: 6.14. Program to compute factorial of a number using recursion.

```python
# This program computes the factorial of a number using recursion

#function definition
def fact(n):
        'computes factorial using recursion'
        if(n==0):
                return(1)
```

```
        else:
                return(n*fact(n-1))


# Function call
num=input('enter a number:')
num=int(num)
result=fact(num)
print('factorial=',result)
```

Output

enter a number:6
factorial=720

fact(6)	# 1st call with 6
6 * fact(5)	# 2nd call with 5
6*5*fact(4)	# 3rd call with 4
6*5*4*fact(3)	# 4th call with 3
6*5*4*3*fact(2)	# 5th call with 2
6*5*4*3*2*fact(1)	# 6th call with 1
6*5*4*3*2*1	# return from 6th call with value 1
6*5*4*3*2	# return from 5th call
6*5*4*6	# return from 4th call
6*5*24	# return from 3rd call
6*120	# return from 2nd call
720	# return from 1st call

Fig. 6.2. Factorial computation using recursive calls.

6.8.1. Advantages of Recursion

- Recursive functions divide the problem into smaller similar fragments and then computes them.
- The recursive code looks precise and cleaner as compared to using loops.
- Sequence generation is simpler in recursion such as Fibonacci series as compared to that of loops.

6.8.2. Disadvantages of Recursion

- Recursive code is hard to develop and debug as it involves huge complexity.
- Difficult to understand.
- Recursive functions are expensive as numerous calls occur within the function, which takes up lot of memory space and time.
- Recursive function are slower than iterations (loops).

6.9. Scope and Lifetime of Variables

The scope of a variable can either be local or global. It is region of the program, where it is recognized. If a variable is defined outside all the functions of a program then its scope is considered to be global. As the value of that variable can be accessed by any of the functions. Such a variable is termed as global variable. On the other hand, the local variable exhibits a limited scope. Any variable defined inside a function is referred to as a local variable as it can be accessed only within that function.

The lifetime of a variable is the duration or period for its existence in the memory. The lifetime of a local variable is as long as that function executes. They are destroyed or removed from the memory once function is returned back to the function call. On the other hand, the lifetime of a global variable is as long as the whole program executes.

The program given in Code: 6.15. illustrates the concept of local and global variables. In this program, we see that a variable val is defined globally with value 0. A function call scope(10) is made with the argument 10. From the output, it is perceived that inside the function definition of scope() it prints 10 and after the function call it prints 0. It apparently signifies that the scope of variable val inside function definition is local whereas after the function call statement the val is printed out to be 0 , i.e., the value is taken up from the global variable.

Code: 6.15. Illustration of global and local variables.

```
# This program illustrates local and global variables

val=0  # global variable defined
#fucntion definition
```

```
def scope(val):
        'local variable illustration'
        print(val)
        return


#function call
scope(10)
print(val)
```

Output
10 0

6.10. Summary

In this chapter, we have learned about one of the best constructs of Python programming language known as functions. The two types of functions built-in and user defined are described. As Python supports a huge library of built-in functions a complete list is provided with the description of each. Subsequently, user defined functions are explained in depth with their various types along with the illustration of each. Anonymous functions, which are developed with lambda function are elaborated in detail. The Python pass by value and pass by object reference are also described with their respective illustrations. One of the most exciting type of functions known as recursion is described. In the end, the chapter concludes with describing the scope and lifetime of variables.

Review Questions

Q.1   What is meant by function in Python language? What is their need and advantages?

Q.2   Write down the types of functions provided by Python language. with an illustration of each.

Q.3   How will you distinguish built-in functions and user defined functions?

Q.4   Write down the procedure to write a user defined function in Python.

Q.5   What are different forms of user defined functions provided by Python language?

Q.6   Elaborate functions with no arguments with example.

Q.7   Elaborate functions with arguments with example.

Q.8   Write down the significance of return statement in Python. Is it mandatory to write return statement in every function definition?

Q.9   What is the significance of anonymous functions provided by Python?

Q.10   Illustrate the lambda function with an appropriate example.

Q.11   What do you understand by recursion? What are its advantages and disadvantages?

Q.12   Explain recursion with the help of a suitable programming language.

Q.13   Distinguish call by value and call by reference in Python with an appropriate programming example.

Q.14   How will you distinguish local and global variables used in Python?

Q.15   Explain scope and lifetime of variables of Python variables.

Programming Exercises

Develop following programs by user defined functions

1. Write a program to compute simple and compound interest.
2. Write a program to design a simple calculator.
3. Write a program to compute sum of first N natural numbers.
4. Write a program to generate a Fibonacci series.
5. Write a program that determines whether a number is prime or not.
6. Write a program to print prime numbers between certain interval.
7. Write a program to compute mean, variance, and, standard deviation.
8. Write a program to compute factorial of a number.
9. Write a program to print a multiplication table.
10. Write a program to compute sum of A. P. series.
11. Write a program to compute sum of G. P. series.
12. Write a program to compute sum of H. P. series.
13. Write a program to compute area of following shapes
    a. Triangle
    b. Circle
    c. Rhombus
    d. Parallelogram

e. Trapezium

14. Write a program to print Fibonacci series using recursion.
15. Write a program to compute GCD using recursion.
16. Write a program to print tower of Hanoi using recursion.
17. Write a program to compute the binomial coefficient ^nC_r.
18. Write a program to print day of a month.
19. Write a program to illustrate the use of filter () function with the support of lambda function.
20. Write a program to evaluate the following expressions

a. $x - \dfrac{x^3}{3!} + \dfrac{x^5}{5!} - \dfrac{x^7}{7!} + \dots \dfrac{x^n}{n!}$

b. $x - \dfrac{x^2}{2!} + \dfrac{x^3}{3!} - \dfrac{x^4}{4!} + \dots \dfrac{x^n}{n!}$

21. Write a program to display a calendar.
22. Write a program to shuffle a deck of cards.
23. Write a program to convert decimal number to equivalent binary, octal, and hexadecimal numbers.
24. Write a program to print ASCII value of a number or character.

CHAPTER 7

Python Modules

Highlights

- Python modules
- Creating modules
- Importing modules
- Standard modules
- Python packages

In the previous chapter, we have learnt about the creation of Python user defined functions. We have seen that a large problem can be divided into small fragments to solve each of them separately using functions. In this chapter, we study about modules, which is an extension to the user defined functions. As in C, C++, and Java header files or packages are used to make use of built-in functions, in Python modules are used to utilize built-in Python functions. Apart from that, similar to C/C++/Java, where user can create header files or packages to use them similar to built-in ones, Python has the feature to create modules for further use.

7.1. Need of Module

In interpreter based Python programming language, all the definitions, variables, and functions written by the programmer gets lost, when he quits the interpreter. However, another way to save the program code is to write the program in a script form in some editor such as notepad, which we have followed so far in this book. For large programs, it is a good practice to divide it into several files for better understanding and maintenance. Moreover, sometimes similar function is used in multiple programs, so rather than writing the same code again and again it is a good practice to make it a module and use it in different programs.

To support this, Python has the distinct feature of module in which a programmer can put definitions in a file and use them in a script or in an interactive instance of the interpreter. The definitions written inside a module can be imported into the main module by using the import command.

Another major role of module is to provide reusability of code. As mostly used function definitions can be written inside a module and be used several times without writing the similar code repetitively.

7.2. Module Definition

A module can be defined with some function definitions and statements. The file name is the module name or it can be same as the task it performs with an extension .py. For example, if we wish to design a module which computes factorial then its name can be factorial.py.

| **Note** | It is to be noted that the module file must be saved in the same directory, where main program resides or where it will be imported. |

7.3. Creating a Module

In this section, we will demonstrate the creation of a module. A module is created as a script file, which contains function definitions that can be called in two ways

- From the interpreter

- From another script file or from another function

Now, we shall discuss both the above ways of module importing in detail. As we know that factorial is the most frequently used operation and needs to be computed repeatedly in many programs. Here, we will create a module named fact.py, which computes the factorial of a number. Consider the program given in Code 7.1. This program contains only the definition of the function factorial(), where n is passed as an argument.

Code: 7.1. Illustration of module fact containing definition of factorial().

```python
# This program illustrates the designing/creation of a module

def factorial(n):
        "This module computes factorial"
        f=1;
        for i in range (1, n+1):
                f=f*i;
        print(f)
        return
```

7.4. Importing Module in the Interpreter

The module given in Code 7.1. is saved as fact.py in the same directory where Python interpreter is located. Now, in the interpreter mode we just import the fact module and then make a call to factorial() to achieve the operation. The interpreter mode is given in Fig. 7.1. We see from the figure that factorial() is called four times after importing the fact module and provides the intended output.

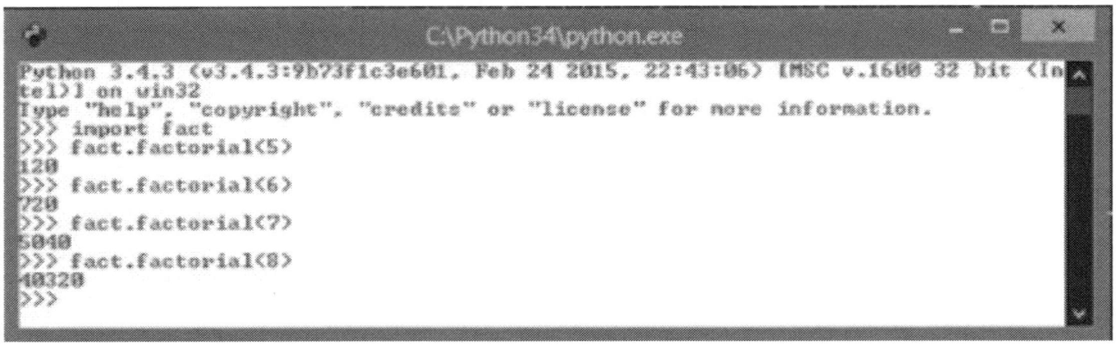

Fig. 7.1. Output of importing and calling fact module in interpreter mode.

7.5. Importing Module in Another Script

Let us assume, we need to compute the sum of the following series

$$\frac{1}{1!} + \frac{2}{2!} - \frac{3}{3!} + \ldots + \frac{n}{n!}$$

In this series, the programmer needs to compute the factorial n times. Thus, we will reuse the already created module fact.py and import it inside another script which computes the sum of above series. The program of module is given in Code 7.2. It slightly differs from the Code 7.1., in that it returns the value of the computed factorial to the script written in Code: 7.3., where it has been imported. Note that this module given in Code. 7.3. must be saved in the same directory where module fact.py is saved.

Code: 7.2. The illustration of module fact, which returns the value of computed factorial.

```
# This program illustrates the designing/ creation of a module

def factorial(n):
        "This module computes factorial"
        f=1;
        for i in range (1, n+1):
                f=f*i;
        return f
```

Code: 7.3. The computation of given series by importing fact module.

```
# To compute a series 1/1!+2/2!+3/3!+...+n/n!

import fact
n=input('enter number:')
n=int(n)
sum=0.0
for i in range (1, n+1):
        sum=sum+(i/fact.factorial(i))
print('sum=',sum)
```

Output

```
enter number: 7
sum= 2.7180555555555554
```

In the code 7.3., we see that the fact module is imported by using the import statement. Subsequently, fact.factorial(i) statement is used to call the factorial() function written inside the fact.py module. Finally, the computed sum is displayed by using the print statement.

Another example of module is given in Code 7.4., which is used to display a Fibonacci series. Two functions have been defined in this module. First function fib() prints the values of the computed Fibonacci series. However, other function fibo() returns the computed Fibonacci series as a list to the calling script. The import in interpreter mode is displayed in Fig. 7.2. We can see that Fibonacci module is imported by using the import command. Then function fib() is called three times with arguments 1000, 100, and 10 , and the intended result is obtained.The Python script importing and calling the module Fibonacci is given in Code: 7.5. In script mode, we see that the number n upto which user wish to display Fibonacci series is asked from the user. Then n is passed as an argument to the appropriate function defined inside the module Fibonacci using the statement fibonacci.fibo(n). The Fibonacci module is imported in the script by the import statement. From the output, we see that the intended result is obtained.

It is to be noted that in the Fibonacci module two functions are defined fib() and fibo(). The function fib() is called in the interpreter mode to achieve the result, whereas fibo() is called in script mode. The user can call any of the defined functionsfib() and fibo() either in interpreter mode, i.e., at Python prompt or in script mode.

Code: 7.4. The illustration of module Fibonacci, used to print Fibonacci series upto n.

```
# To compute a Fibonacci series 0 1 1 2 3 5 8 11.....

def fib(n):
        'this prints the fibonacci series upto n'
        a=0
        b=1
        c=0
        while(c<n):
                print(c, end=' ')
                c=a+b
                a=b
                b=c
        return

deffibo(n):
        'this returns the fibonacci series as a list upto n'
        a=0
        b=1
        c=0
        fib_series=[]
```

```
        while(c<n):
                fib_series.append(c)
                c=a+b
                a=b
                b=c
        return fib_series
```

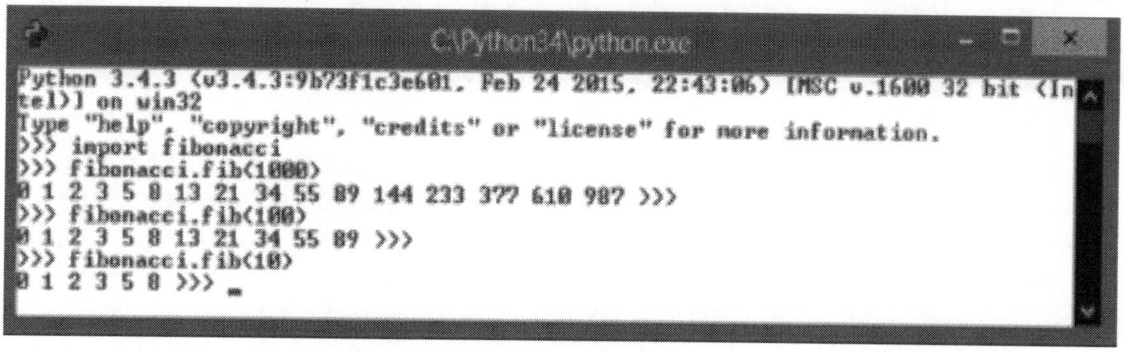

Fig. 7.2. Interpreter mode call to Fibonacci module

Code: 7.5. Python script to import and call Fibonacci series

```
# To compute a Fibonacci series 0 1 1 2 3 5 8 11..... through module

import fibonacci

n=input('enter n:')
n=int(n)
print(fibonacci.fibo(n))
```

Output

```
enter n:1000
[0, 1, 2, 3, 5, 8, 13, 21, 34, 55, 89, 144, 233, 377, 610, 987]
```

7.6. Importing Modules

From the above sections, we see that the statements defined inside a module can be imported inside another module or at Python prompt of the interactive Python interpreter. The import statement is used to achieve this task. 'import' is a keyword followed by module name to be imported. In the above programming examples, we import the fact module at Python prompt as follows

```
>>> import fact
```

The above statement does not include all the functions defined inside the fact module. However, it only inserts the module name. This imported or inserted module then can be used to call any function defined inside its script using the dot(.) operator. For example, the function factorial() can be called from the module fact as follows:

```
>>>fact.factorial(10)
```

A particular function definition or a name from a module can be called using the from import statement. In the Code 7.3., we see that two function definitions fib() and fibo() have been defined in the script of module Fibonacci. A specific function let's assume fibo() can be imported as follows

```
import fibo() from fibonacci
```

By using the above statement only the fibo() function is imported from the Fibonacci module. Thus, in the calling script the programmer needs to write only fibo(n) rather than Fibonacci.fibo(n) statement as shown in Code: 7.5. One can import all the function definitions of a module by using the * (asterisk) operator as follows

```
import * from fibonacci
```

By using the above statement, both fib() and fibo() functions are imported in the module Fibonacci. Thus, user can access their definitions directly without using the dot(.) operator. However, for good programming practice, importing everything with the asterisk (*) symbol should be avoided. This can lead to duplicate definitions for an identifier. It also impedes the readability of the code.

7.7. Search Path of Module

When a module is imported either in interactive mode or script mode, the Python searches the path of module at various places. The interpreter initially looks for the built-in modules. In case of user created modules, the search order of interpreter works as follows:

- The current directory

- The path set in the environment variable (PYTHONPATH)

- The default directory sys.path

7.8. Module Reloading

The Python interpreter imports a module only once in a session. If some modifications are performed in the module script then it must be reloaded (imported) again in the interpreter for further use. This can be illustrated through an example. Consider the Fig. 7.1., where the module fact has been imported to call factorial() function. If the programmer makes some changes in the definition of factorial() then the fact module needs to be imported again in the interpreter otherwise it will provide the last executed output. One way is to call the import command again on the prompt as import fact or restart the interpreter. The other way is to call the reload() function, which is defined inside the imp module. This can be done as follows

```
>>> import imp

>>>imp.reload(fact)
```

7.9. The dir() Function

In order to see the list of function names defined in a module, Python is provided with a built-in function called dir(). It displays the list of all the function definition names as follows

```
>>>dir(fibonacci)

['__builtins__', '__cached__', '__doc__', '__file__', '__loader__',
'__name__', '__package__', '__spec__','fib']
```

From above, we see a sorted list of names with the user created definition fib is displayed as the output. The names begin with an underscore _ are default Python attributes with the module. They are associated by themselves by Python while creating a module. By calling empty dir() results as follows

```
>>>dir()

['__builtins__', '__cached__', '__doc__', '__file__', '__loader__',
'__name__', '__package__', '__spec__', 'fibonacci']
```

It shows that it provides the module name Fibonacci with the built-in files rather than providing the function definition names as no module name is passed as an argument to dir().

7.10. Standard Modules

The Python language comprises with a library of standard modules. Some of them are available on the interpreter, which provide access to operations that are not part of the core of the language. Such modules are used to make system calls or to provide access to operating system. One of the important system module sys, is available on Python interpreter. The variable sys.path is a list of strings that determines the search path for modules. Usually, it is initialized to default path taken from the environment variable PYTHONPATH. This can be modified by using standard list operations. The list of built-in standard modules can be seen in Appendix-I.

7.11. Python Packages

As we see in Windows, all the files are stored in a hierarchical fashion. This feature is provided to organize the files to access them later on efficiently rather than searching them here and there. Similar kinds of files are placed in the same directory. For example, pictures are stored in the directory called photos or pictures. Music files can be stored in directory names songs or music. Similarly, video files are stored in a video directory.

Analogous to above, when a program becomes larger, we can divide it in different modules as described in the above sections. Python provides packages for managing directories and modules for files. Similar modules can be placed in one package, which makes maintenance of the project or program under development easier. As directory can contain sub directories, similarly a package can contain sub packages.

The directory containing package must contain a file named __init__.py. This is required as Python identifies it as a package due to __init.py__ file. This file can be empty or we place the initialization code for the package to execute.

For example, we wish create a package shape which contains modules as follows in Code 7.6. In this code, we see that a package shape is created at top level, which contains two sub-packages shape_2D and shape_3D. The __init.py__ file is written in the code to initialize the package above it. It can be seen that shape_2D contains two modules area.py and perimeter.py to compute these operations for 2D shapes. Whereas, shape_3D package contains volume.py and surface_area.py modules to compute these operations for 3D shapes.

Code:7.6. Creation of a package shape.

```
# package shape
shape/                    #Top level package
     __init.py__          #Initializing the shape package
     shape_2D/            #sub-package for 2D shape
```

```
            __init.py__        #Initializing the shape package
        area.py
        perimeter.py
    shape_3D/              #sub-package for 3D shape
            __init.py__        #Initializing the shape package
        voulme.py
        surface_area.py
```

A particular package can be called by using the import statement, as we have done for built-in packages. In the above package, the shape module can be called as follows

```
import shape
```

The above statement will import all the sub packages as well as modules described in shape package. A particular sub package can be called as follows

```
import shape.shape_2D
```

The above statement will import shape_2D package and all the modules defined inside it. A particular module can be imported from a package or sub package using the from keyword as follows

```
from shape.shape_2D import area
```

It is to be noted that, while importing packages, Python looks in the list of directories in sys.path.

7.12. Summary

In this chapter, we have learned the creation of modules, which is an extension of user defined functions described in the previous chapter. We discussed need, definition and creation of modules in detail. Importing of a module in interpreter as well as script mode is described with examples. The searching path of modules and dir() function is described. The built in standard modules are also discussed. At the end of the chapter, the creation of packages and their use is discussed.

Review Questions

Q.1 What are modules? Why are they needed in Python?

Q.2 Design a module in Python by giving an example.

Q.3 What are the different ways to import a module? Explain each method with appropriate example of each.

Q.4 What is the significance of import command? Give programming example.

Q.5 How will you determine the search path of a module?

Q.6 What is the purpose of dir() function with respect to modules.

Q.7 List some of the standard modules available in Python with their respective description.

Q.8 What are packages? Why are they needed? Explain the hierarchy of packages with the help of an appropriate example.

Programming Exercises

1. Write a program to illustrate the creation of a module and importing it through interpreter mode.
2. Write a program to illustrate the creation of a module and importing it in a Python script file.
3. Illustrate the creation and use of package by an appropriate program.

CHAPTER 8

Exception Handling

Highlights

- Python exceptions
- Built-in exceptions
- Exception handling
- Try, except, finally
- User defined exceptions

While writing a Python code, certain errors may occur. In the first place, these errors can prevent the program from being executed by the interpreter. These errors are called compile time errors. For an instance, forgetting to follow exact syntax of a particular construct such as if statement or making a spelling mistake, missing a semicolon or colon, may cause interpreter/compile time error. The program gets executed only after these errors are rectified. Let us consider a program given in Code 8.1. This program determines whether a number is even. In the if statement, we see that colon (:) is missing. The execution of this code raises a syntax error as presented in Fig. 8.1.

Code: 8.1. Illustration of interpreter time error (syntax error).

```
# This program illustrates syntax error

number=input('Enter a number:')
number=int(number)
if number%2==0
        print('Number is even')
print('out of if block')
```

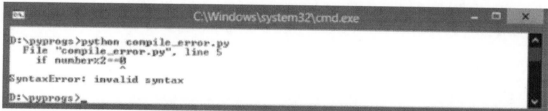

Fig. 8.1. Output of Code 8.1

8.1. Exception

There exists some errors which occur at run time in the program. For instance, attempting to divide by zero or accessing a list, which is not defined, opening a file that does not exist are common examples of run time errors. The run time error is called exception. By the occurrence of these errors, Python creates an exception object. If not handled properly, it prints a traceback to that error along with some details about why that error has occurred. For instance, consider a simple code given in Code: 8.2. We see that there is no syntax error in this code, therefore, it executes without any error. The output of this code is given in Fig. 8.2., we see if the user inputs the value of number as 0 then the expression c=15/number evaluates to c=15/0, then due to division by zero, ZeroDivisionError exception occurs and we don't obtain the output.

Code: 8.2. Illustration of runtime error (Exception).

```
# This program illustrates run time error

number=input('Enter a number:')
number=int(number)
c=15/number
print(c)
```

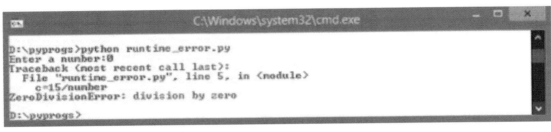

Fig. 8.2. Output of Code 8.2

8.2. Python Built-in Exceptions

Python language detects exceptions if they occur during the execution of a program. There exists numerous built-in Python exceptions listed in Table 8.1. with the description of each.

Exception	Cause
AssertionError	Raised when assert statement fails.
AttributeError	Raised when attribute assignment or reference fails.
EOFError	Raised when the input() functions hits end-of-file condition.

FloatingPointError	Raised when a floating point operation fails.
GeneratorExit	Raise when a generator's close() method is called.
ImportError	Raised when the imported module is not found.
IndexError	Raised when index of a sequence is out of range.
KeyError	Raised when a key is not found in a dictionary.
KeyboardInterrupt	Raised when the user hits interrupt key (Ctrl+c or delete).
MemoryError	Raised when an operation runs out of memory.
NameError	Raised when a variable is not found in local or global scope.
NotImplementedError	Raised by abstract methods.
OSError	Raised when system operation causes system related error.
OverflowError	Raised when result of an arithmetic operation is too large to be represented.
ReferenceError	Raised when a weak reference proxy is used to access a garbage collected referent.
RuntimeError	Raised when an error does not fall under any other category.
StopIteration	Raised by next() function to indicate that there is no further item to be returned by iterator.
SyntaxError	Raised by parser when syntax error is encountered.
IndentationError	Raised when there is incorrect indentation.
TabError	Raised when indentation consists of inconsistent tabs and spaces.
SystemError	Raised when interpreter detects internal error.
SystemExit	Raised by sys.exit() function.
TypeError	Raised when a function or operation is applied to an object of incorrect type.
UnboundLocalError	Raised when a reference is made to a local variable in a function or method, but no value has been bound to that variable.
UnicodeError	Raised when a Unicode-related encoding or decoding error occurs.
UnicodeEncodeError	Raised when a Unicode-related error occurs during encoding.
UnicodeDecodeError	Raised when a Unicode-related error occurs during decoding.

UnicodeTranslateError	Raised when a Unicode-related error occurs during translating.
ValueError	Raised when a function gets argument of correct type but improper value.
ZeroDivisionError	Raised when second operand of division or modulo operation is zero.

Table 8.1. Python Built-in Exceptions

8.3. Exception Handling

When an exception occurs, the current process stops and passes it to the calling process until it is handled to obtain the result. If not handled properly, the program crashes and the intended output is not obtained and the program comes to a halt.

8.3.1. Try, Except, and Finally

In Java, try and catch blocks are used to handle exceptions, in Python, exceptions can be handled using a try and except statements. A critical operation which can raise exception is included in the try clause and the code for handling the exception is included in except clause. Consider a programming example in Code: 8.3. In this program, we see that the user is asked to input an integer number and then its reciprocal will be computed. In the output, we see that if user enters a character or float (real) value then ValueError exception occurs, which is caught by the except clause and the appropriate error message "please try again" along with exception is displayed to the user. The while loop executes until the user supplies a valid integer value as an input for the computation of valid reciprocal. The critical portion that can cause exception is placed inside the try block. If there is no exception then programs executes with normal flow and if error occurs then it is caught by the except clause. Therefore, we see exception occurs three times for inputting a, 1.5, and 0 and handled by the except block of the program by providing value error and divide by zero error messages. In the code exc_info module is used to fetch the type of exception from the sys module. Therefore, sys module is necessary to import in this program.

Code: 8.3. Illustration of Try and Except clauses.

```
# This program illustrates to handle exceptions using try and except
clauses

import sys

while True:
  try:
    x = int(input("Enter an integer: "))
    r = 1/x
    break
  except:
print("Oops!",sys.exc_info()[0],"occured.")
print("Please try again.")
    print()

print("The reciprocal of",x,"is",r)
```

Output

Enter an integer:a
Oops! <class 'ValueError'>occured.
Please try again.

Enter an integer:1.5
Oops! <class 'ValueError'>occured.
Please try again.

Enter an integer:0
Oops! <class 'ZeroDivisionError'>occured.
Please try again.

Enter an integer:5
The reciprocal of 5 is 0.2

8.3.2. Catching Specific Exceptions in Python

We can also handle exceptions separately rather than all exceptions in one block. In Python, a try clause can have multiple except clauses just like a try block can have multiple catch blocks in Java. Only one of them will be executed depending upon the type of occurred exception. The code for the same is illustrated in Code 8.4.

Code: 8.4. Illustration of multiple except clauses.

```
try:
    # do something
    pass

except ValueError:
    # handle ValueError exception
    pass

except (TypeError, ZeroDivisionError):
    # handle multiple exceptions
    # TypeError and ZeroDivisionError
    pass

except:
    # handle all other exceptions
    pass
```

8.3.3. try...finally

As we have seen that the try statement can have multiple except statements. Alike Java, Python also exhibit an optional clause 'finally'. It gets executed automatically, and is mostly used to release external resources. For example, while developing some large projects, we may be connected to a server on the network or to a file of GUI. Then in such situations, to release all the resources finally exception clause can be used. It will ensure that all resources are freed up to guarantee successful execution of the program. The program illustrating the same is displayed in Code 8.5.

Code: 8.5. Illustration of finally clause.

```
try:
fp = open("check.txt",encoding = 'utf-8')
  # perform file operations
finally:
fp.close()
```

Note: This type of construct makes sure the file is closed even if an exception occurs.

8.4. Python User-Defined Exceptions

In Python, users can create their own exceptions. This can be done by creating a new class which is derived from the Exception class. It is to be noted that most of the built in exceptions are also derived from the Exception class. On the Python prompt, a user defined exception can be created as follows as shown in Code 8.6. We see that a user defined exception NewException is created which is derived from the Exception class. This NewException can be raised just like other existing exceptions by using the raise statement with an optional error message.

Code: 8.6. Illustration of user defined exception NewException.

```
>>> class NewException(Exception):
...     pass
...

>>> raise NewException
Traceback (most recent call last):
...
__main__.NewException

>>> raise NewException("An error has occurred")
Traceback (most recent call last):
...
__main__.NewException:An error has occurred
```

An illustration of user defined exception is given in Code: 8.7. This program presents a number game, where user has to guess a number. If user enters a number greater than the saved number then message is displayed as number is too large, otherwise message is displayed as number is too small. This process continues until the user guesses the correct number. All this process is handled through user defined exception. Here, a base class Guess is created derived from the built-in Exception class. Consequently, two derived classes ValueTooSmall and ValueTooLarge are created, inherited from Guess class.

Code: 8.7. Illustration of number game using user defined exception.

```
# define Python user-defined exceptions
class Guess(Exception):
  """Base class for other exceptions"""
  pass

class ValueTooSmall(Guess):
  """Raised when the input value is too small"""
  pass

class ValueTooLarge(Guess):
  """Raised when the input value is too large"""
  pass

# our main program, where user guesses a number until he/she gets it right
# user needs to guess this number

number = 10

while True:
  try:
i_num = int(input("Enter a number: "))
    if i_num< number:
      raise ValueTooSmall
elifi_num> number:
      raise ValueTooLarge
    break
  except ValueTooSmall:
```

```
    print("This value is too small, try again!")
        print()
      except ValueTooLarge:
    print("This value is too large, try again!")
        print()

    print("Congratulations! You guessed it correctly.")
```

Output
Enter a number: 7
This value is too small, try again!

Enter a number: 20
This value is too large, try again!

Enter a number: 4
This value is too small, try again!

Enter a number: 9
This value is too small, try again!

Enter a number: 11
This value is too large, try again!

Enter a number: 10
Congratulations! You guessed it correctly.

8.5. Summary

In this chapter, we have discussed about interpreting time errors (syntax errors) and run time errors. Run time errors are also called exceptions. Various built-in exceptions are available in Python language. However, user can create his own exceptions for handling different circumstances, which can occur during the execution of the program. All exception handling constructs try, except, finally are discussed with the programming illustration of each of them. User defined exceptions are also discussed with example.

Review Questions

1. What is an Exception? How it differs from errors in Python?

2. How exception is declared and defined in Python? Illustrate with an example.
3. What are built-in exceptions? List built-in exceptions with the purpose of each.
4. What do you understand by Try, Except and Finally in Python?
5. How try..except works in Python? Illustrate with a program.
6. How try...finally works in Python? Illustrate with a program.
7. What are user defined exceptions? How they differ from built-in exceptions?
8. How user defined exceptions are defined and used in Python? Give a suitable programming example.

CHAPTER 9

File Management in Python

Highlights

- Python files
- Operations on files
- File modes, File encoding
- write() and read() methods
- Python file methods
- Renaming and deleting files
- Python directories
- Python directory methods

In all the programs that we have developed so far using Python language, we see that the output is lost when we exit from the program. However, in certain situations, it is necessary to save the data for future use. This can be achieved by making use of files. File is a place on the disk with certain name to store related information. This information is stored on the secondary storage memory known as hard disk, flash drive, etc. However, if we do not store the data on the hard disk in the form of a file, then it resides in the computer's primary memory RAM (Random Access Memory). The RAM is a volatile memory which loses its data, when the computer is turned off. However, hard disk is a permanent storage and also called as non-volatile memory.

A computer programmer or data entry operator always prefers to enter the data in the files instead of storing the data in a temporary storage. This is done for the following reasons:

1. The complete data will be lost, if either the system is turned off or power failure occurs.
2. Repetition of same data entry will be a time consuming process.
3. It is cumbersome to enter huge amount of data through the keyboard or any other input device.
4. Data cannot be corrected or updated.
5. The data is unreliable if it needs to enter through the keyboard.
6. In case of an error during the data entry process, the entire process will be started all over again.
7. Problems can also be faced during testing and debugging during the program.
8. Validation and verification of data is not possible without saving it on the file.
9. The reliability of information increases while saving it on the disc as a file.
10. Efficiency of the program also increases.

Therefore, to overcome all the issues listed above files provide a better approach for permanent storage of important and processed information. More precisely, a file is defined as **"A file is a single entity pertains to a collection of related data structure."**

9.1. Operations on Files

Initially, we need to open the file first for reading or writing data into it. After performing operations on the file or saving data into it, it needs to be closed. It is necessary to close the file in order to release the resources acquired by the program. Hence, in Python, a file operation takes place in the following order.

1. Open a file
2. Read or write (perform operation)
3. Close the file

9.1.1. Opening a File

In Python, a file can be opened by open() function. It is a very simple built-in function of Python to open a file. This function creates a file object, which would be utilized to call other support methods associated with it. The general syntax of open method is given as follows:

```
file object= open(file_name,access_mode, buffering)
```

The open() function contains three parameters, which are elaborated as under:

- **file_name:** The file_name argument is a string value that contains the name of the file that the programmer wishes to access.

- **access_mode:** The access_mode determines the mode in which the file has to be opened, i.e., read, write, append, etc. The detail of modes is given in the next section.

- **buffering:** If the buffering value is set to 0, no buffering takes place. If the buffering value is 1, line buffering is performed while accessing a file. If the programmer specifies the buffering value as an integer greater than 1, then buffering action is performed with the indicated buffer size. The negative value of buffer size represents the system default behavior.

Apart from above, the open() function can be used in two ways. In the first way, the programmer just needs to specify the FileName with an optional extension with a period (.). By just specifying the file name in the open() method as an argument, it creates the file in the current directory. Another way is to specify the complete path, where programmer wants to save the file. The output of this function is assigned to a file object, which is used to read, write, or modify the file. The example for opening a file is given in Code 9.1. This method is directly applied on the Python prompt.

Code: 9.1. Illustration of opening a file using Python open() function.

```
>>>fp = open("data.txt")    # open file in current directory
>>>fp= open("C:/Pythonprogs/data.txt")  # specifying full path
```

9.1.2. File Modes

Alike, C, C++, and Java, a file can be opened in various modes depending upon the purpose. For that, the programmer needs to specify the mode whether read 'r', write 'w', or append 'a' mode. Apart from that, two other modes exist, which specify to open the file in text mode or binary mode. The default is reading in text mode. The text mode returns strings while reading from the file. On the other hand, binary mode returns bytes and this is the mode to be used when dealing with non-text files like image or executable files. The text and binary modes are used in conjunction with the r, w, and a modes. The list of all the modes used in Python are listed in Table 9.1.

Mode	Description
r	Opens a file for reading only. The file pointer is placed at the beginning of the file. This is the default mode.
rb	Opens a file for reading only in binary format. The file pointer is placed at the beginning of the file.
r+	Opens a file for both reading and writing. The file pointer placed at the beginning of the file.
rb+	Opens a file for both reading and writing in binary format. The file pointer placed at the beginning of the file.
w	Opens a file for writing only. Overwrites the file if the file exists. If the file does not exist, creates a new file for writing.

wb	Opens a file for writing only in binary format. Overwrites the file if the file exists. If the file does not exist, creates a new file for writing.
w+	Opens a file for both writing and reading. Overwrites the existing file if the file exists. If the file does not exist, creates a new file for reading and writing.
wb+	Opens a file for both writing and reading in binary format. Overwrites the existing file if the file exists. If the file does not exist, creates a new file for reading and writing.
a	Opens a file for appending. The file pointer is at the end of the file if the file exists. That is, the file is in the append mode. If the file does not exist, it creates a new file for writing.
ab	Opens a file for appending in binary format. The file pointer is at the end of the file if the file exists. That is, the file is in the append mode. If the file does not exist, it creates a new file for writing.
a+	Opens a file for both appending and reading. The file pointer is at the end of the file if the file exists. The file opens in the append mode. If the file does not exist, it creates a new file for reading and writing.
'x'	Opens a file for exclusive creation. If the file already exists, the operation fails.
'a'	Opens for appending at the end of the file without truncating it. Creates a new file if it does not exist.
't'	Opens in text mode. (default)
'b'	Opens in binary mode.
'+'	Opens a file for updating (reading and writing)

Table 9.1. File opening modes.

The example code for opening a file in particular mode is given in Code: 9.2.

Code: 9.2. Illustration of opening a file in a particular mode.

```
fp = open("data.txt")      # equivalent to 'r' or 'rt'
fp = open("data.txt",'w')  # write in text mode
fp = open("img.jpg",'r+b') # read and write in binary mode
```

9.1.3. File Object Attributes

After opening a file, the programmer can access information about the file using various available attributes. The list of attributes is given in Table 9.2. with the description of each. the use of attributes is explained in Code 9.3.

Attribute	Description
fp.closed	Returns true if file is closed, false otherwise.
fp.mode	Returns access mode with which file was opened.
fp.name	Returns name of the file.
fp.softspace	Returns false if space explicitly required with print, true otherwise.
Note: fp is the file object.	

Table 9.2. Python file attributes.

Code: 9.3. Illustration of file attributes.

```
# This program creates a file and prints its attributes

# Open a file
fp = open("data.txt", "wb")
print ('Name of the file: ', fp.name)
print ('Closed or not : ', fp.closed)
print ('Opening mode : ', fp.mode)
```

```
Output

Name of the file:  data.txt
Closed or not :  False
Opening mode :  wb
```

9.1.4. File Encoding

In Python version 3.x and above the encoding of files is made clear. Here, with encoding we mean either text mode or binary mode. Unlike other languages C and C++, the character 'a' does not imply the number 97 until it is encoded using ASCII(or other equivalent encodings). Hence, when working with files in text mode, it is recommended to specify the encoding type. Files are stored in bytes on the disk, we need to decode them into str (text) when we read into Python. Similarly, encoding is performed while writing texts to the file. The default encoding depends on the platform whether Windows or Linux. The encoding scheme for Windows is 'cp1252' and 'utf-8' is used in Linux. Hence, one must not rely on the default encoding otherwise, the code can behave absurdly in different platforms. Thus, this is the preferred way to open a file for reading in text mode as shown in Code 9.4.

Code: 9.4. Illustration of file encoding.

```
fp= open("test.txt",mode = 'r',encoding = 'cp1252')  # for Windows
fp= open("test.txt",mode = 'r',encoding = 'utf-8')  # for Linux
```

9.1.5. Closing a File

In Python, the file can be closed by using the close() function. It is a built-in function provided by Python for manually closing a file and releasing all the resources acquired by it. Python automatically closes a file, when the reference object of file is assigned to another file. However, it is a good programming practice to close the file using the close() function. The general syntax of close() function is given as follows:

```
fileobject.close();
```

The programming example of closing a file is given in Code 9.5.

Code: 9.5. Illustration of closing a file.

```
# This program creates and closes a file after printing its attributes

# Open a file
fp = open("data.txt", "wb")
print ('Name of the file: ', fp.name)
print ('Closed or not : ', fp.closed)
print ('Opening mode : ', fp.mode)
fp.close();
```

```
Output

Name of the file:  data.txt
Closed or not :  False
Opening mode :  wb
```

This method is not entirely safe. If an exception occurs when we are performing some operation on the file, the code exits without closing the file. A safer way is to use a try...finally block as shown in Code 9.6.

Code: 9.6. Illustration of closing a file using try... finally (exception handling).

```
try:
fp = open("data.txt",encoding = 'utf-8')
   # perform file operations
finally:
fp.close()
```

This way, we are guaranteed that the file is properly closed even if an exception is raised, causing program flow to stop.

9.2. write () and read() Methods

Alike, C, C++, and Java, data can be written and read from the file by using some methods in Python. For writing data into the file write() method is used. However, for reading data from the file read() method is used. These methods are very easy to use in Python and described in the following sub sections.

9.2.1. Writing to a File

In order to perform write operation on a file, it must be opened first in either write mode 'w', append mode 'a', or exclusive mode 'x'. While opening a file in 'w' mode, some caution is required. If file to be opened already exists then it will overwrite the contents of the file. That means, all the previous contents of the file will be lost or erased. Writing data to the file is accomplished by using write() method. This method returns the number of characters written to the file. The syntax of write() method is given as follows:

```
fileObject.write(string)
```

Code: 9.7. Illustration of write() method.

```
# Illustration of write() method

with open("data.txt",'w',encoding = 'cp1252') as fp:
fp.write("This is an illustration \n")
fp.write("of writing\n")
fp.write("data to the file\n")
fp.close();
```

The program presented in Code 9.7 shows that how data is written to the file. This program creates a new file named 'data.txt' if it does not exist. If it already exists, it is overwritten. In order to differentiate different lines newline character (\n) can be used as shown in the program. Since, we are working in Windows, 'cp1252' encoding is used while opening the file. After performing writing operation on the file using the write() method, file is closed through the file object and close() function. We see that 'with' clause used with the open() function for opening the file, this is done to avoid the occurrence of any exception during the execution of the program. This is an alternate of using try ... finally clause, as described in the previous section.

9.2.2. Reading from a File

In the previous section, we have learnt how to write data into the file. Now, we will learn how to read the contents of a file. This can be accomplished by using the read() method. But, before that the file must be opened in read mode 'r'. The syntax of read() method is given as follows:

```
fileObject.read(size)
```

In the above syntax, we see that size argument is specified in the read() method. It determines the number of characters to be read by the method. If the size is not mentioned, then it reads and returns all the characters upto end of file. The illustration of using read() method is presented in Code 9.8. In this program, we read the data, which was written to a data.txt file in the previous program given in Code 9.7. Initially, the file is opened in the read mode 'r' and with windows encoding scheme. Then data is read character by character by specifying its size. This method inserts newline character by itself after reading specified number of characters. In order to read the entire line or whole text at one go, the read() method can be used without specifying the number of characters in the argument as done in the second last line of code in the program.

Code:9.8. Illustration of read() method.

```
# illustration of read() method

with open("data.txt",'r',encoding = 'cp1252') as fp:
   print(fp.read(5))
   print(fp.read(5))
   print(fp.read())
fp.close();
```

```
Output

This
is an
 illustration
of writing
data to the file
```

Another method of reading the contents of a file is by using readline(). The example of this method is given in code 9.9. We see from the program that the readline() method reads and returns the entire line as written into the file. When EOF (end of file) is reached, it returns the empty string. If programmer wishes to read and print the entire file at one time, then readlines() method can be used. It reads all the lines and returns to the user. The program for the same is given in Code 9.10.

Code: 9.9. Illustration of readline() method.

```
# illustration of readline() method

with open("data.txt",'r',encoding = 'cp1252') as fp:
   print(fp.readline())
   print(fp.readline())
   print(fp.readline())
   print(fp.readline())
fp.close();
```

Output

This is an illustration

of writing

data to the file

Code: 9.10. Illustration of readlines() method.

```
# illustration of readline() method

with open("data.txt",'r',encoding = 'cp1252') as fp:
   print(fp.readlines())
fp.close();
```

Output

['This is an illustration \n', 'of writing\n', 'data to the file\n']

Another way is to read the contents of file by using the for loop. This method is easier and efficient than the read() and readline() methods. The illustration for reading a file using for loop is given in Code: 9.11.

Code: 9.11. Illustration of reading a file using for loop.

```
# illustration of reading a file using for loop

with open("data.txt",'r',encoding = 'cp1252') as fp:
        for line in fp:
                print(line)
fp.close();
```

Output

This is an illustration

of writing

data to the file

9.3. Python File Methods

Python provides various methods associated with files to work with. These methods are used in conjunction with file object. The list of file methods is given in Table 9.4. Some of these methods have been illustrated in the previous sections.

Method	Description
close()	Closes an open file. It has no effect if the file is already closed.
detach()	Separates the underlying binary buffer from the TextIOBase and return it.
fileno()	Returns an integer number (file descriptor) of the file.
flush()	Flushes the write buffer of the file stream.
isatty()	Returns True if the file stream is interactive.
read(n)	Readsatmost n characters form the file. Reads till end of file if it is negative or None.
readable()	Returns True if the file stream can be read from.

readline(n=-1)	Reads and return one line from the file. Reads in at most n bytes if specified.
readlines(n=-1)	Reads and return a list of lines from the file. Reads in at most nbytes/characters if specified.
seek(offset,from=SEEK_SET)	Changes the file position to offsetbytes, in reference to from (start, current, end).
seekable()	Returns True if the file stream supports random access.
tell()	Returns the current file location.
truncate(size=None)	Resizes the file stream to size bytes. If size is not specified, resize to current location.
writable()	Returns True if the file stream can be written to.
write(s)	Writes string s to the file and return the number of characters written.
writelines(lines)	Writes a list of lines to the file.
Note: All these methods are used with the fileobject. E.g. fp.close(), where fp is the file object.	

Table 9.4. Python File Methods

9.4. tell() and seek() Methods

tell(): This method is used to determine the current position of a file pointer. It can be used either while writing to a file or reading from the file. The syntax of tell is given as follows:

```
fileObject.tell()
```

seek(): This method is used to move the file pointer to a particular location in the file. The syntax for seek() is given in as follows:

```
seek(offset [, from])
```

In the above syntax, the offset represents the number of bytes to be moved from the specified position. The from argument represents the reference position from where the bytes are to be relocated. The value of from can be one of the values given in Table 9.5.

from	value
Beginning	0
Current	1
End	2

Table: 9.5. Reference positions of from offset

The programming illustration of tell() and seek() methods is given in Code 9.12. In this program, we see that tell(), tells the current position of the file and seek() is reading the file from the current position.

Code: 9.12. Illustration of tell() and seek() methods.

```
# Illustration of tell() and seek() methods

with open("data.txt",'r',encoding = 'cp1252') as fp:
print(fp.read(4))
pos=fp.tell()
print('Current Position:', pos)
fp.seek(0, 1)
print(fp.readline())
fp.close();
```

```
Output

This
Current Position: 4
is an illustration
```

9.5. Renaming and Deleting Files

Python language provides special methods for renaming and deleting a file. These methods are available through the Python os module. For using these methods, the programmer needs to import the os module. Both of these methods are very easy to use and described below:

9.5.1. rename() method

The rename() method takes two arguments. The syntax of rename() method is given as follows:

```
os.rename(old_file_name, new_file_name)
```

The programing example for using the rename() is given in Code 9.13. We see that the data.txt file already exists. By using the rename() method, it is renamed to info.txt. The programmer can see in the current directory that the file has been renamed.

Code: 9.13. Illustration of rename() method.

```
#Illustration of renaming a file

Import os
os.rename('data.txt', 'info.txt')
```

9.5.2. remove() method

The remove() method is used to delete the file. It has only one argument, which is the file name to be deleted. The syntax of remove() is given as follows:

```
os.remove(file_name)
```

The programming example for using the remove() method is given in Code 9.14. This program removes the file from the current directory. After the execution of this program the programmer can see that the file will not be present in the current directory and can be obtained from the recycle bin.

Code: 9.14. Illustration of remove method.

```
# Illustration of deleting a file

import os
os.remove('info.txt')
```

9.6. Directories in Python

So far, we have discussed the creation of files in Python and various operations upon them. However, we can also work on directories in Python. This is achieved by making use of os module and various methods in it. Here, we discuss all the methods associated with the directories in Python.

9.6.1. mkdir() method

The mkdir() method is used to create directories in the current directory. This method contains only one argument that is the name of the directory to be created. The syntax for using the mkdir is given as follows

```
os.mkdir("new_directory_name")
```

The programming example of mkdir() is presented in Code 9.15. After the execution of this program a new directory datafiles is created in the current folder.

Code: 9.15. Illustration of mkdir() method.

```
# Illustration of creating a directory

Import os
os.mkdir('datafiles')
```

9.6.2. chdir() method

The chdir() method is used to change the current directory. It also takes one argument for moving from one directory to another and making it the current directory. The general syntax of chdir is given as follows:

```
os.chdir('newdirectory')
```

The programming example representing the use of chdir is presented in Code: 9.16. In this code, we see that initially we create a file new directory "newfiles" inside the existing directory "datafiles" by using the mkdir() method. Then, we change the directory control to the newly created directory "newfiles" by using the chdir() method. Subsequently, we create a new file "input.txt" in write mode and write a message into it. The programmer can see in the parent directory that a new directory "newfiles" and a new file "input.txt" are created.

Code: 9.16. Illustration of chdir() method.

```
# illustration of changing a directory

import os

os.mkdir('datafiles/newfiles');
os.chdir('datafiles/newfiles');
fp=open('input.txt', 'w')
fp.write('Hello, Welcome to Programming in Python')
fp.close()
```

9.6.3. getcwd() method

The getcwd() method is used to obtain the information of the presently working directory. The general syntax of getcwd() is given as below

```
os.getcwd()
```

The programming example of getcwd is given in Code 9.17. In this program, we see that initially, we get the information about current working directory using getcwd() method. Then, we change the directory to datafiles and then by using getcwd() we get the path of the presently working directory. Subsequently, we again change the directory to newfiles and new location of the currently working directory is printed.

Code: 9.17. Illustration of getcwd() method.

```
# illustration of changing a directory

import os

print(os.getcwd())
os.chdir('datafiles')
```

233

```
print(os.getcwd())
os.chdir('newfiles')
print(os.getcwd())
```

```
Output

D:\pyprogs
D:\pyprogs\datafiles
D:\pyprogs\datafiles\newfiles
```

9.6.4. rmdir() method

The rmdir() method is used to remove or delete the directory, which is mentioned in its argument. The general syntax of rmdir() is given as below:

```
os.rmdir('directoryname')
```

The programming example of rmdir() method is given in Code 9.18. In this program, we delete the directory, which was created in Code 9.15. For this, first we need to change the directory to datafiles to make it the presently working directory. Then, the method rmdir() is executed to delete the newfiles directory.

Code: 9.18. Illustration of rmdir() method.

```
# Illustration of changing a directory

import os

os.chdir('datafiles')
os.rmdir('newfiles')
```

9.6.5. listdir() method

The listdir() method is used to get the list of all files and directories in the currently working directory. The syntax for listdir() is given as follows:

```
os.listdir()
```

The programming example for listdir() is given in Code 9.19. This program lists all the files present in the currently working directory.

Code: 9.19. Illustration of listdir() method.

```
# Illustration of listdir() method

import os

print(os.listdir())
```

Output

```
['break_for.py', 'break_while.py', 'chdir.py', 'check.py',
'compile_error.py', 'constant.py', 'continue.py', 'customexception.py',
'datafiles', 'exception1.py', 'fact.py', 'factorial.py', 'fibonacci.py',
'fileattri.py', 'for_read_file.py', 'func.py', 'func_default_arg.py',
'func_keyword_arg.py', 'func_noarg.py', 'func_noarg1.py',
'func_product.py', 'func_rearg1.py', 'func_rearg1_return.py',
'func_var_length.py', 'f_series.py', 'getcwd.py', 'lambda.py', 'listdir.py',
'local_global.py', 'math_func.py', 'mkdir.py', 'nested_for.py', 'output.txt',
'pass.py', 'pass_by_ref.py', 'pass_by_ref1.py', 'pass_by_val.py', 'rand.py',
'readlines_file.py', 'readline_file.py', 'read_file.py', 'recur_fact.py',
'remove.py', 'rename.py', 'rmdir.py', 'runtime_error.py', 'series.py',
'tell_seek_file.py', 'test.py', 'trigono.py', 'userexception.py', 'write_file.py',
'__pycache__']
```

9.7. Python Directory Methods

In the previous section, we have described various Python directory handling methods with the programming illustration of each. However, Python contains a large number of methods to be work with the directories. All these methods are to be used with the os module. That means, the os module needs to be imported for using any of the methods associated with directories. The list of methods to be used with directories is given in Table 9.6. with the description of each method.

Method	Description
os.access(path, mode)	Uses the real uid/gid to test for access to path.
os.chdir(path)	Changes the current working directory to path
os.chflags(path, flags)	Sets the flags of path to the numeric flags.
os.chmod(path, mode)	Changes the mode of path to the numeric mode.
os.chown(path, uid, gid)	Changes the owner and group id of path to the numeric uid and gid.
os.chroot(path)	Changes the root directory of the current process to path.
os.close(fd)	Closes file descriptor fd.
os.closerange(fd_low, fd_high)	Closes all file descriptors from fd_low (inclusive) to fd_high (exclusive), ignoring errors.
os.dup(fd)	Returns a duplicate of file descriptor fd.
os.dup2(fd, fd2)	Duplicates file descriptor fd to fd2, closing the latter first if necessary.
os.fchdir(fd)	Changes the current working directory to the directory represented by the file descriptor fd.
os.fchmod(fd, mode)	Changes the mode of the file given by fd to the numeric mode.
os.fchown(fd, uid, gid)	Changes the owner and group id of the file given by fd to the numeric uid and gid.
os.fdatasync(fd)	Forces write of file with filedescriptorfd to disk.
os.getcwd()	Returns a string representing the current working directory.
os.getcwdu()	Returns a Unicode object representing the current working directory.
os.link(src, dst)	Creates a hard link pointing to src named dst.
os.listdir(path)	Returns a list containing the names of the entries in the directory given by path.
os.lseek(fd, pos, how)	Sets the current position of file descriptor fd to position pos, modified by how.
os.major(device)	Extracts the device major number from a raw device number.
os.minor(device)	Extracts the device minor number from a raw device number .

os.mkdir(path[, mode])	Creates a directory named path with numeric mode mode.
os.remove(path)	Removes the file path.
os.rename(src, dst)	Renames the file or directory src to dst.
os.renames(old, new)	Recursive directory or file renaming function.
os.rmdir(path)	Removes the directory path
os.read(fd, n)	Reads at most n bytes from file descriptor fd. Return a string containing the bytes read. If the end of the file referred to by fd has been reached, an empty string is returned.
os.write(fd, str)	Writes the string str to file descriptor fd. Return the number of bytes actually written.
Note: All these methods are used with the os module. e.g. os.rmdir().	

Table 9.6. Python directories methods

9.8. Summary

In this chapter, we have discussed about data files in detail. Various methods of file and directory handling in Python are discussed with the programming implication of each. The file creation, opening and closing is discussed with various modes of operation such as reading and writing to a file. Apart from that file renaming, deleting, making directory, changing directory, and removing directory methods are discussed.

Review Questions

Q.1 What are files? What is the significance of using files in Python?
Q.2 How would you create a file? Write the syntax of open() method.
Q.3 Write a program to open a file in Python.
Q.4 What are various file opening modes available in Python? Describe each mode.
Q.5 List the operations that you can perform on files?
Q.6 Describe various attributes associated with the file object.
Q.7 Elaborate encoding techniques linked with files.
Q.8 How would you close a file in Python?
Q.9 Explain the significance of write() and read() methods in Python with the programming example of each.
Q.10 Distinguish read(), readline(), and readlines() methods in Python.
Q.11 How would you read the data from a file in Python using for loop?

Q.12   List all the methods associated with files in Python with the description of each.

Q.13   Elaborate the use of tell() and seek() methods in Python.

Q.14   How would you rename and delete a file in Python?

Q.15   Explain the following with programming example of each
   a.   mkdir()
   b.   chdir()
   c.   rmdir()
   d.   listdir()
   e.   getcwd()

Q.16   List all the methods applicable on directories in Python with the description of each.

Q.17   What is the purpose of os module in Python while using files and directories?

Q.18   What is the significance of file object in Python?

Programming Exercises

1. Write a program to create a file which stores the following information of n students:
    Name, RollNo, Name of 5 subjects, and Marks of 5 subjects.

2. Write a program to open the file created in Program 1 and compute the total marks and grade of all the students then display and save total marks and grade along with Name, RollNo, Marks, etc in the pre-existing file.

3. Write a program to a file named Invoice of purchased items from a general store, which contains ItemNo, ItemName, Price, Quantity. Compute the total_bill then display and save the file along with preexisting data.

4. Write a program to create a file containing the information of patients of a hospital with attributes PatientName, PatientID, Age, Gender, Disease, Status(Cured or Not Cured) and Contact Number.

5. Write a program to create a file exhibiting the data of a bank account with details, CustomerName, AccountNo, AccountType, Balance, and Contact Number.

6. Write a program to create a file containing the record of employees with attributes Employee_Name, Emp_ID, Department, Basic_Pay, Total_Salary (Basic+DA+HRA+MA), where DA is 125% of

Basic_Pay, HRA is 20% of Basic_Pay, MA is 10% of Basic_Pay. Computes the total salary and save the complete record of 10 employees in the file.

CHAPTER 10

Classes and Objects

Highlights

- Designing classes
- Creating objects
- Accessing attributes
- Built-in class attributes
- Garbage collection

Object oriented is a term used to describe the object oriented approach for building software. In an object oriented approach, the data is treated as the most important element and it cannot flow freely around the system. This approach binds the data and the methods that will manipulate the data closely and prevents the data from being modified inadvertently. The object oriented programming exhibits following properties:

1. Encapsulation
2. Data hiding and abstraction
3. Inheritance
4. Polymorphism (overloading/overriding)
5. Dynamic binding

Here we will discuss each of this property in brief.

Encapsulation: The wrapping of data and functions into a single unit is known as encapsulation.

Data hiding and abstraction: It refers to represent the necessary features without including the background particulars.

Inheritance: It refers to the property by which objects of one class inherit the properties of objects of another class.

Polymorphism: It refers to the ability to take more than one form. Here poly means many and morphism means forms. For example, the addition of two numbers will result into sum however, the addition of two strings results into concatenation of strings. That means to use single operator + for different purposes refers to operator overloading.

Dynamic binding: It refers to the linking of procedure call to the code to be executed in response to the call. Dynamic binding means that the code associated with a given procedure call is not known until the time of the call at run-time.

Alike Java, Python is also an object oriented programming language. It possesses all the properties as described above. Before indulging in concepts in great details the basic object oriented programming (OOP) terminology is given as follows:

- **Class:** A user-defined prototype defines a set of attributes that describe any object of the class. The attributes are data members (class variables and instance variables) and methods, accessed via dot notation.

- **Class variable:** A variable that is mutually shared by all instances (objects) of a class. Class variables are defined within a class but outside any of the class's methods.

- **Method:** A special kind of function that is defined in a class definition.

- **Instance variable or Data member:** A class variable or instance variable that holds data associated with a class and its objects or an individual object of a certain class. For example, an object obj that belongs to a class Triangle is an instance of the class Triangle.

- **Instantiation:** The creation of an instance of a class.

- **Object:** A unique instance of the user defined data type class. An object comprises of both data members (class variables and instance variables) and methods.

10.1. Designing Classes

The class is a basic major entity of object oriented programming language. A class can be defined by using the keyword "class". The general syntax of defining a class in Python is as follows:

```
class ClassName:
        'documentation string"
        class details
```

In the above syntax, we see that class is defined by using the keyword class with the ClassName, which is to be kept by the programmer and the naming conventions are same as that applied on identifiers. Similar to functions the class statement is followed by an optional documentation string that keeps the information about the class being created. After that the complete details of the class are given, where class variables, data members and methods can be created and used. The programming instance of using a class is presented in Code 10.1.

Code: 10.1. Illustration of creating a class in Python.

```
#Illustration of creating a class in Python

class Student:
    'A student class'                #documentation string
    stuCount = 0                     #class variable

    def __init__(self, name, rollno):   #initialization or constructor method
                                        #of class Student
        self.name = name
        self.rollno = rollno

        Student.stuCount += 1

    def displayCount(self):          #displayCount method of class Student
        print ("Total Students %d", Student.stuCount)

    def displayStudent(self):            #displayStudent method of class
                                         #Student
        print ("Name : ", self.name,  ", Rollno: ", self.rollno)
```

In this Python programming code, we see that a class is created with the name Student, which contains a class variable stuCount and its value will be shared by all the instances (objects) of the class. Then a method __init__() is created, which is special class method known as class constructor or the initialization method. This method is called automatically when a new instance of a class is created. Two more class methods displayCount() and displayStudent() are also created with an argument self. In Python, it is mandatory to write self as an argument to a class method or function. However, while calling this function, the self is not passed as an argument.

10.2. Creating Objects

As mentioned earlier, the instance of a class is called object. Creating an object in Python is very simple. The syntax of defining an object is given as follows:

```
ObjName=ClassName(arglist)
```

where, the argument list can be the values to be supplied to the data members of the class through constructor. The example for creating objects of the class Student given in Code 10.1. is given as in Code 10.2.

Code: 10.2. Illustration of creating objects

```
stu1=Student('John', 111)        # first object of class Student
stu2=Student('Clara', 112)       #second object of class Student
```

10.3. Accessing Attributes

In Python, the attributes of a class can be accessed by using the dot(.) operator, as in C++ and Java. For example, for the above class Student of Code 10.1. the class methods displayCount() and displayStudent() can be accessed outside the class as shown in Code 10.3.

Code: 10.3. Illustration of accessing class methods and class variable

```
stu1.displayStudent()
stu2.display.Student()
Student.stuCount
```

10.4. The Class Program

The complete program representing the entire concept of creating classes and objects is given in Code 10.4. Here we see that a class variable stuCount is created and two data members i.e., name and rollno are created. The values to name and rollno are assigned through the constructor method __init__() in Python. It contains three arguments. The first is the self, which is mandatory in Python for every function (method) to be used within class. The other two arguments are name and rollno.

Two class methods displayCount() and displayStudent() are also defined to display the total number of students and information of the students. Then, two objects stu1 and stu2 and created with the values of name and rollno, which are passed as argument to the constructor function. Subsequently, displayStudent() method is called through stu1 and stu2 objects by using the dot(.) operator. The value of common class variable stuCount is displayed or accessed by using the class name with the variable name stuCount along with dot operator. The output of this code explains it all.

Code: 10.4. Illustration of using classes and objects in Python.

```
#Illustration of creating a class in Python

class Student:
  'A student class'
  stuCount = 0

  def __init__(self, name, rollno):   #initialization or constructor method
of                                    #class Student
    self.name = name
    self.rollno = rollno
    Student.stuCount += 1

  def displayCount(self):     #displayCount method of class Student
    print ("Total Students %d", Student.stuCount)

  def displayStudent(self):          #displayStduent method of class
                                     #Student
    print ("Name : ", self.name,  ", Rollno: ", self.rollno)


stu1=Student('John', 111)
stu2=Student('Clara', 112)
stu1.displayStudent()
stu2.displayStudent()
print('total no. of students:', Student.stuCount)
```

Output

```
Name :  John , Rollno:  111
Name :  Clara , Rollno:  112
total no. of students: 2
```

10.4.1. Using a Class with Input

In the above program, we have seen that the __init__() method is used as a constructor to pass values to the class attributes name and rollno. What if the user wishes to give his/her input for the attributes? In order to understand this concept, consider a program given in Code 10.5. for the same class Student.

Code: 10.5. Illustration of class with input from the user.

```
#Illustration of creating a class in Python with input from the user


class Student:
    'A student class'
    stuCount = 0
    def __init__(self):         #initialization or constructor method of
                                #class Student
        self.name=input('enter student name:')
        self.rollno=input('enter student rollno:')
        Student.stuCount += 1

    def displayStudent(self): #displayStduent method of class Student
        print ("Name : ", self.name,  ", Rollno: ", self.rollno)


stu1=Student()
stu2=Student()
stu3=Student()
stu1.displayStudent()
stu2.displayStudent()
stu3.displayStudent()
print('total no. of students:', Student.stuCount)
```

Output

```
enter student name:John
enter student rollno:21
enter student name:Clara
enter student rollno:122
enter student name:Richie
enter student rollno:123
Name :  John , Rollno:  121
Name :  Clara , Rollno:  122
Name :  Richie , Rollno:  123
total no. of students: 3
```

It is to be noted that while using class in Python, the __init__() method is mandatory to be called for declaring the class data members, without which we can not declare the instance variables(data members) for the objects of the class. A variable declared outside the __init__() method are termed as class variables such as stuCount variable in the above program. It is to be noted that the class variables are accessed as className.classVariableName, e.g. Student.stuCount in the above program. However, the instance variables or data members are accessed as self.instanceVariableName, e.g., self. Name in the above program 10.5.

In this program, we see that the input() function is called in the definition of __init__() method for inputting the values of data variables name and rollno. Subsequently, the value of stuCount is incremented by 1 in order to keep track of total number of objects created for the class Student. In this program, three objects stu1, stu2, and stu3 are created thereby calling the constructor function __init__() three times. The values are assigned to name and rollno after inputting from the user. Then, the result is displayed by calling the displayStudent() function of class Student. The output of this program can be referred for more lucidity.

10.4.2. A Class Program with Computations

Here, we present another program using the concept of class and objects. We create a class inventory and computes the total price of each item along with total bill of all the purchased items. The programming example for this problem is given in Code 10.6.

Code: 10.6. Managing inventory using classes.

```
#Illustration of creating and handling Inventory using class

class Inventory:
    'An inventory class'
    itemCount = 0
    total_bill = 0

    def __init__(self, item, price, quantity):  #constructor method of
                                                #class Inventory
        self.item = item
        self.price = price
        self.quantity = quantity
        self.total = self.price * self.quantity
        Inventory.total_bill += self.total
        Inventory.itemCount += 1


    def displayItem(self):                       #displayStudent method of
                                                #class Inventory
        print ("\nItemName : ", self.item,  "\nPrice: ", self.price, "\nQuantity:
", self.quantity, "\nTotal:", self.total)


I1=Inventory('Soap', 30.5, 4)
I2=Inventory('Shampoo', 130.5, 2)
I3=Inventory('Oil', 80.5, 1)
I1.displayItem()
I2.displayItem()
I3.displayItem()
print('\ntotal no. of items:', Inventory.itemCount)
print('\ntotal bill:', Inventory.total_bill)
```
Output

```
ItemName :  Soap
Price:  30.5
Quantity:  4
Total: 122.0

ItemName :  Shampoo
Price:  130.5
Quantity:  2
Total: 261.0

ItemName :  Oil
Price:  80.5
Quantity:  1
Total: 80.5

total no. of items: 3

total bill: 463.5
```

In this program, we create two class variables itemCount and total_bill and initialized them to zero. Three class instance variables are created, item, quantity, and, price. The value of them are initialized using the __int__() method. In the __init__ method, we perform computations for total price and total_bill. The displayItem() function displays the details of all the items. Outside the class template, we create three objects I1, I2, and I3 by passing values of three items. Then displayItem() function is called three times for all three objects. Subsequently, total itemCount and total bill is displayed. User can see the output for more lucidity.

While using the concepts of classes and objects one must consider the following points:

- The __init__() method is mandatory while using all the classes in Python. It is a constructor method used for instantiation of the object. This method is called implicitly when an object of a class is created.

- All the methods and functions used inside classes of Python language contains an obligatory argument "self". The argument self as it suggests, refers to *itself*- the object which has called the method. That is, if you have N objects calling the method, then self.a refers to a separate instance of the variable for each of the N objects.
- The variables declared inside the __int__() method are data members or instance variables of the class, whereas variables declared outside the __init__() method are called class variables.
- The class variables can be thought of as static variables as in C, C++, and Java. The class variables exhibit the similar properties as that of a static variable. By virtue of which, they are used to count the number of instances created for a particular class. That means the value of class variables persist between different methods/function calls.
- The class variables are accessed outside the class definition by using the className then dot(.) operator and classVariableName, e.g., className.classVariableName.
- The data members and member functions of a class are accessed with the object name, dot operator and variable name or method name, e.g., ObjectName.DataMemberName or ObjectName.MethodName
- The class template begins with the class keyword, then all the details of a class begins with indentation. At the end, the unindented mark of class represents the complete definition or exit from the class template.
- Unlike C++ or Java, Python does not require the main() function for declaring objects of classes. Only the unidented mark represents that the user can create objects and use them.

10.5. Editing Class Attributes

Unlike C++ and Java in Python, the programmer can add, delete or modify class attributes. It is very simple procedure, which can be performed by using the class object name with the class attribute by using the dot (.) operator. For example, in the above program given in Code 10.6, where inventory class is created with attributes item, price, quantity, and total bill. Any of these attributes can be modified or deleted. Moreover, one can also add an additional attribute. The programming example for the same is given in Code

10.7. In this program, we add a new attribute code by using the class object I1.code=111, then we modify the value of "price" attribute by assigning the new value as I1.price=29 then we display the values of new attributes by calling the function displayItem(), which provides the output as shown in output section of Code 10.7. Finally, the deletion of any of the attribute can be performed by del keyword. It is just a keyword to delete the reference of certain attribute of a class. In the code given in 10.7., we delete the code attribute as del I1.code. We observe from this code that it is very easy to add, delete, or modify any of the attribute of a class in Python. However, other languages such as C++ and Java do not offer such provision.

Code: 10.7. Illustration of adding, deleting, modifying class attributes.

```
#Illustration of adding, modifying, and deleting class attributes

class Inventory:
  'An inventory class'
  itemCount = 0
  total_bill = 0

  def __init__(self, item, price, quantity):   #initialization or constructor
                                               #method of class Inventory
    self.item = item
    self.price = price
    self.quantity = quantity
    self.total = self.price * self.quantity
    Inventory.total_bill += self.total
    Inventory.itemCount += 1


  def displayItem(self):    #displayStudent method of class Inventory
    print ("\nItemName : ", self.item, "\nPrice: ", self.price, "\nQuantity: ", self.quantity, "\ncode:", self.code, "\nTotal:", self.total)


I1=Inventory('Soap', 30.5, 4)
I1.code=111              # addition of a new attribute code
I1.price=29.0            # modifying the value of price attribute
I1. displayItem()        # displaying the updated values of I1 object
del I1.code              # deleting an attribute code
```
Output

```
ItemName :  Soap
Price:  29.0
Quantity:  4
code: 111
Total: 122.0
```

Apart from the above the Python language provides certain methods to obtain information about class attributes. The information for these functions is given in Table 10.1 and the programming code is given in Code 10.8. In this program, we see that the Python built-in functions are also very easy to use to obtain information about certain attributes or to set or modify new values or deleting the reference of an object. The output of Code 10.8. makes it all apparent.

Method	Description
getattr(obj, name[, default])	to obtain or access the value of attribute of a class
hasattr(obj,name)	to determine whether an attribute exists or not (results in true or false)
setattr(obj,name,value)	to set the value of an attribute. If attribute does not exist, then it would be created with value
delattr(obj, name)	to delete an attribute

Table 10.1. Built-in class functions

Code: 10.8. Illustration of adding, modifying, and deleting class attributes using built-in Python functions

```python
#Illustration of adding, modifying, and deleting class attributes using
built-in functions

class Inventory:
    'An inventory class'
    itemCount = 0
    total_bill = 0

    def __init__(self, item, price, quantity): #initialization or constructor
                                                #method of class Inventory
        self.item = item
        self.price = price
        self.quantity = quantity
```

```
        self.total = self.price * self.quantity
        Inventory.total_bill += self.total
        Inventory.itemCount += 1


    def displayItem(self):    #displayStudent method of class Inventory
        print ("\nItemName : ", self.item,  "\nPrice: ", self.price, "\nQuantity:
", self.quantity, "\ncode:", self.code, "\nTotal:", self.total)



I1=Inventory('Soap', 30.5, 4)
print(hasattr(I1, 'code'))      # determines whether 'code' attribute exists or
not
print(getattr(I1, 'item'))      # obtains the value of 'item' attribute
setattr(I1, 'price',35)         # sets the new value of 'price' attribute
setattr(I1, 'code', 111)        # sets (creates) a new attribute 'code' which is
                                # not pre-existed
I1. displayItem()               # displays the value of all the attributes of class
                                # inventory
delattr(I1, 'code')             # deletes 'code' attribute
```

Output

```
False
Soap

ItemName :  Soap
Price:  35.0
Quantity:  4
code: 111
Total: 122.0
```

10.6. Built-in Class Attributes

We have seen in the previous sections that how to create a class and attributes of a class. As, we know that class is a user defined data type. The programmer can create his own data type in the form a class, which follows the concept of object oriented programing structures. While creating a class, we specify our own attributes. However, certain attributes intrinsically associated with the class, when it is created. The list of built-in attributes is given in Table 10.2. with the description of each. The programming example for the same is given in Code 10.9. As we can see from the program that the first built-in attribute __dict__ gives the information about the class variables itemCount and total_bill and class functions displayItem(), __init__() along with other details. The __doc__ attribute gives the information about the document string which is "An inventory class" for this code. Subsequently, the __name__ module provides the class name which is 'inventory'. __module__ gives the __main__ module. At the end, the __bases__ attribute gives the "(<class 'object'>,)" since there is no base for this class. It is to be noted that the class built-in attributes are accessed with the classname, dot (.) operator and attribute not with the object of the class as in the previous code given in 10.8.

Attribute	Description
__dict__	Dictionary containing the class's namespace
__doc__	Class documentation string or none, if undefined
__name__	Class name
__module__	Module name in which the class is defined. This attribute is "__main__" in interactive mode.
__bases__	A possibly empty tuple containing the base classes, in the order of their occurrence in the base class list.

Table 10.2. Python built-in class attributes

Code: 10.9. Illustration of using built-in class attributes

```
#Illustration of using built-in class attributes

class Inventory:
  'An inventory class'
```

```
      itemCount = 0
      total_bill = 0

      def __init__(self, item, price, quantity):    #initialization        or
      constructor                                    #method  of  class
      Inventory
         self.item = item
         self.price = price
         self.quantity = quantity
         self.total = self.price * self.quantity
         Inventory.total_bill += self.total
         Inventory.itemCount += 1


      def displayItem(self):                         #displayStudent method of
                                                     #class Inventory
         print ("\nItemName : ", self.item,  "\nPrice: ", self.price, "\nQuantity:
      ", self.quantity, "\ncode:", self.code, "\nTotal:", self.total)


   I1=Inventory('Soap', 30.5, 4)
   print(Inventory.__dict__)
   print('\n')
   print(Inventory.__doc__)
   print('\n')
   print(Inventory.__name__)
   print('\n')
   print(Inventory.__module__)
   print('\n')
   print(Inventory.__bases__)
```

Output

```
{'__weakref__': <attribute '__weakref__' of 'Inventory' objects>,
'__dict__': <attribute '__dict__' of 'Inventory' objects>, '__init__':
<function Inventory.__init__ at 0x02D03390>, '__doc__': 'An inventory
class', 'total_bill': 122.0, 'displayItem': <function Inventory.displayItem at
0x02D034B0>, '__module__': '__main__', 'itemCount': 1}

An inventory class
```

```
Inventory

__main__

(<class 'object'>,)
```

10.7. Garbage Collection/Destroying Objects

Python facilitates the destruction of objects automatically when certain object's reference count reaches zero. That means Python deletes class instances automatically to free the memory space so that it can be utilized by some other program. The process of automatically and periodically cleaning the blocks of memory that is no longer required is called as garbage collection. The garbage collector works automatically in the background to frees up any dereferenced space of memory. An object reference count increases when it is assigned a new name or place in a container and object reference count decreases when it is deleted with the del statement as in the previous example Code 10.7.

As the garbage collector works automatically, we do not know in the front end when an object has been destroyed by garbage collector. However, Python provides a special method __del__(), called a destructor, that is called when the instance is about to be destroyed. The syntax of destructor method __del__() is given as follows:

```
def __del__(self):
```

We see from the syntax that it contains self as the argument followed by colon (:), i.e., function definition similar to the other class methods. The programming code to understand this concept is given in Code 10.10. From the output of the code it is apparent that when we create an object the class method __init__() is invoked automatically and when we delete the instance of a class then the class method __del__() is invoked. In this program, we create three objects I1, I2, and I3 of the class inventory. When the first object is created it calls the __init__() method to assign attributes to the object I1. We increment the value of class variable itemCount in the __init__() method and print the message that "No. of object created 1". Similarly when second call occurs when I2 object is created the __init__() method increments and prints the message as "No. of objects created 2". Likewise, in case of the third object I3, the message "No. of object created 3" will be displayed.

Now we delete the reference of these three objects by using the *del* statement. On the occurrence of *del I1* the class method __del__() is invoked where the value of class variable itemCount is decremented by 1 and the message is printed as "No. of object destroyed 3". Subsequently while deleting I2, and I3 objects the __del__() method is invoked and prints the messages as "No. of object destroyed 2" and "No. of object destroyed 1" for I2 and I3 respectively. By this way, all the objects are deleted by the Python garbage collector. Although the garbage collector of Python sweeps the memory automatically, by using the class method __del__() the procedure of destruction of objects can be understood effectively.

Code: 10.10. Illustration of destructor method __del__()

```
#Illustration of destroying of objects using destructor method __del__()

class Inventory:
  'An inventory class'
  itemCount = 0

  def __init__(self, item, code, price, quantity): #initialization or
                                      #constructor method
    self.item = item
    self.code = code
    self.price = price
    self.quantity = quantity
    Inventory.itemCount += 1
    print('No. of object created', Inventory.itemCount)

  def __del__(self):        #destructor method of class Inventory
    Inventory.itemCount -= 1
    print('No. of object destroyed', Inventory.itemCount)

  def displayItem(self):    #displayStudent method of class Inventory
    print ("\nItemName : ", self.item, "\nPrice: ", self.price, "\nQuantity:
", self.quantity, "\ncode:", self.code, "\nTotal:", self.total)
```

```
I1=Inventory('Soap', 'SP111', 30.5, 4)
I2=Inventory('Shampoo', 'SO312', 130.5, 2)
I3=Inventory('Oil', 'OL232', 80.5, 1)
del I1
del I2
del I3
```
Output

No. of object created 1

No. of object created 2

No. of object created 3

No. of object destroyed 2

No. of object destroyed 1

No. of object destroyed 0

10.8. Summary

In this chapter, we have discussed one of the significant concept in programming, i.e., object oriented programming structures in Python. We learn the creation of classes and objects. The constructor method __init__() of Python is described, which is used to initialize the class members. The process to access class members is also discussed. The concept of using classes is demonstrated in detail by various programming illustrations. The built-in methods to be used within classes are also discussed. The destructor method __del__() to frees up memory space is also discussed.

Review Questions

Q.1   What do you understand by object oriented programming structures (OOPS)? List and describe the features of OOPS.

Q.2   How to create and use classes and objects in Python? Illustrate with a programming example.

Q.3   How the data members and class functions of a class are accessed in Python?

Q.4   Differentiate between class methods and class functions with example.

Q.5   How a user can modify or edit class attributes? What are various functions to perform this operation? Explain with programming example.

Q.6   List Python built-in class attributes with the description of each.

Q.7   What is a destructor? How to deallocate memory space occupied by object in Python? Elaborate.

Programming Exercises

1.   Write a program to create a class BankAccount, which contains the data members account_number, customer_name, account_type, balance and class methods deposit(), withdraw(), and summary(). Include an option that a user can withdraw a maximum amount of rupess 10000/- per transaction and the balance must meet the minimum balance amount of rupees 1000/- in the account.

2.   Write a program to create a class Employee containing the data members emp_name, emp_ID, Dept, basic_pay, HRA, DA, MA with member functions total_salary() [computes the total salary based on basic pay, HRA=20% of basic_pay, DA=120% of basic_pay, and MA=5% of basic_pay] and emp_details, displays the complete details of the employee.

3.   Write a program to create a class Electricity_bill with data members bill_id, customer_name, meter_no, no_of_units, total_amount, previous_balance and member functions compute_bill(), which computes the monthly electricity bill based on the following criteria:

Units	Cost per unit (Rs.)
200	5/-
200-400	7/-
400-800	10/-
800-1600	13/-
Above 1600	15/-

If the previous bill is not paid then previous bill along with penalty will be added to the current bill. The complete details must be displayed by the display() function of the class.

CHAPTER 11

Python Inheritance

Highlights

- Inheritance
- Single, multiple, multilevel
- Method overriding
- Special functions in Python

In the previous chapter, we have learnt the designing of classes and objects in Python. Reusability or inheritance is one of the most significant features of OOPS. It is a good practice to reuse something which already exists rather than creating the new one all over again. It would not save only time and energy but also increases the reliability, as the already build code is previously tested and debugged. Alike, C++ and Java, Python classes also use the concept of inheritance. Inheritance enables us to define a class that takes all the functionality and features of the base class. The base class is known as the parent class or super class and the derived class is also known as the child class or subclass. Here in this section, we will learn the concept of using inheritance in detail. The general syntax of using inheritance is given as follows:

```
class DerivedClass(BaseClass):
        Body of Derived Class
```

The above syntax is quite simpler than that is used in C++ and Java for inheriting classes. The DerivedClass represents the new class and the BaseClass represents the old class followed by a colon. The body of the class begins with indentation. The inheritance can be categorized into single inheritance, multiple inheritance, and multilevel inheritance. Each of them is described in the following sections.

11.1. Python Single Inheritance

A program to represent the concept of single inheritance is displayed in Code 11.1. In this program, we create a base class shape which contains two data members length and breadth as shown in the constructor method __int__() of the class shape. The base class shape contains one class function display, which displays the values of length and breadth. Then, we create a class rectangle which is inheriting the features of base class shape. By deriving, the members length, breadth and display() of base class shape will become the members of derived class rectangle as well apart from its own members area and compute_area(). Now, we create the object r1 of derived class rectangle and calls the functions display() and compute_area() with the object of rectangle. It is to be noted here that, we have not created the object of base class shape and just by creating the object of derived class rectangle, we can access the data members and functions of the base class.

While the creation of object r1 of derived class rectangle the constructor method __init__() of the derived class rectangle is invoked which further invokes the constructor method of base class shape. The __init__() method of base class shape inputs the values of length and breadth. Subsequently, the base class function display() is called by r1.display(), which displays the values of length and breadth of rectangle. At the end, the derived class function r1.compute_area() is called, which computes the area of rectangle and displays the appropriate result. The output of the code is also given for verification.

Code: 11.1. Illustration of single inheritance.

```python
#Illustration of single inheritance

class shape:                              #base class
    'A shape class'
    def __init__(self):                   #constructor method of base class
        self.length = float(input('Enter Length:'))
        self.breadth = float(input('Enter Breadth:'))

    def display(self):                    #display method of base class
        print ("\nLength: ", self.length)
        print ("\nBreadth: ", self.breadth)

class rectangle(shape):                   #derived class
    'A rectangle class'
    def __init__(self):                   #constructor method of derived class
        shape.__init__(self)
        self.area=0
    def compute_area(self):               #compute_area funciton of derived class
        self.area = self.length*self.breadth
        print("\nArea of rectangle=", self.area)
```

```
r1=rectangle()           # object of derived class
r1.display()
r1.compute_area()
```

Output

Enter Length:6.5
Enter Breadth:7.8
Length: 6.5
Breadth: 7.8
Area of rectangle= 50.699999999999996

11.2. Python Multiple Inheritance

Multiple inheritance refers to two or more base classes and one derived class. In this type of inheritance, the features of multiple classes can be inherited into the derived class. The programming example of multiple inheritance is given in Code 11.2. This program contains three classes, two base classes student and marks and one derived class result, which inherits the traits of both student and marks classes. The student class having two data members name and rollno of student and a class function display, which displays the values of name and rollno. The another base class marks contains three data members m1, m2, and m3 representing marks of three subjects. It also contains a class function display_marks(), which displays the marks of all the three subjects. Now, the third derived class result, which is derived from both the base classes student and marks contains two data members total_marks and perc representing percentage. It also contains a class function display_result() to display total_marks and percentage of a student.

In this program, the object of the derived class result is created as r1. It is to be noted here that by the creation of object r1 the __init__() constructor method of derived class result is invoked automatically, which further invokes the constructor methods of base classes student and marks to initialize or input the values of student name, rollno, and marks of three subjects. Subsequently, the total_marks and percentage is computed in the __init__() method of derived class. Then display(), display_marks(), and, display_result() functions of class student, marks, and result are invoked by using the r1 object of result (derived) class. These functions display the appropriate output on the terminal.

Code: 11.2. Illustration of multiple inheritance.

```
#Illustration of multiple inheritance


class student:                                  #base class 1
  'A student class'
  def __init__(self):                  #constructor method of base class 1
    self.name = (input('Enter Student Name:'))
    self.rollno = int(input('Enter RollNo:'))

  def display(self):                   #display method of base class 1
    print ("\nName: ", self.name)
    print ("\nRollNo: ", self.rollno)

class marks:                                    #base class 2
  'A marks class'
  def __init__(self):                  #constructor method of base class 2
    self.m1 = float(input('Enter marks of subject 1:'))
    self.m2 = float(input('Enter marks of subject 2:'))
    self.m3 = float(input('Enter marks of subject 3:'))
  def display_marks(self):             #display function of base class 2
    print("\nMarks of subject 1=", self.m1)
    print("\nMarks of subject 2=", self.m2)
    print("\nMarks of subject 3=", self.m3)

class result(student, marks):          #derived class
  'A result class'
  def __init__(self):                  #constructor method of derived class
```

```
        student.__init__(self)
        marks.__init__(self)
        self.total_marks = self.m1 + self.m2 + self.m3
        self.perc = self.total_marks*100/300
    def display_result(self):        #display_result function of derived class
        print("\nTotal Marks:", self.total_marks)
        print("\nPercentage:", self.perc)


r1=result()                # object of derived class result
r1.display()
r1.display_marks()
r1.display_result()
```

Output

Enter Student Name: John
Enter RollNo:111
Enter marks of subject 1:44
Enter marks of subject 2:54.5
Enter marks of subject 3:36

Name: John

RollNo: 111

Marks of subject 1= 44.0

Marks of subject 2= 54.5

Marks of subject 3= 36.0

Total Marks: 134.5

Percentage: 44.833333333333336

11.3. Python Multilevel Inheritance

In the concept of multilevel inheritance, we see that a derived class can be further inherited by a new derived class. In other words, the features of base class and a derived class can be inherited by a new derived class. The programming illustration of multilevel inheritance is given in Code 11.3. It is almost similar to the program code given for multiple inheritance, where there were two base classes and one derived class. Herein, multilevel inheritance, we create a base class student with the similar data members and functions as mentioned in the previous example. Then, we derive marks class from the student class that means the marks class inherits the traits of student class. Further, we create a new derived class result, which is inherited from the marks class. Eventually, we have three classes with two levels student->marks->result. Thus, the result class contains the traits of both the classes student as well as marks. Alike, previous program the object of result class is created, by which all the operations are performed like earlier and result is displayed.

Code: 11.3. Illustration of multilevel inheritance.

```python
#Illustration of multilevel inheritance

class student:                          #base class
    'A student class'
    def __init__(self):                 #constructor method of base class
        self.name = (input('Enter Student Name:'))
        self.rollno = int(input('Enter RollNo:'))

    def display(self):                  #display method of base class
        print ("\nName: ", self.name)
        print ("\nRollNo: ", self.rollno)

class marks(student):                   #derived class
    'A marks class'
    def __init__(self):                 #constructor method of derived class
        self.m1 = float(input('Enter marks of subject 1:'))
```

```
    self.m2 = float(input('Enter marks of subject 2:'))
    self.m3 = float(input('Enter marks of subject 3:'))
  def display_marks(self):          #display function of base class 2
    print("\nMarks of subject 1=", self.m1)
    print("\nMarks of subject 2=", self.m2)
    print("\nMarks of subject 3=", self.m3)

class result(marks):                          # new derived class
  'A result class'
  def __init__(self):              #constructor method of new derived class
    student.__init__(self)
    marks.__init__(self)
    self.total_marks = self.m1 + self.m2 + self.m3
    self.perc = self.total_marks*100/300
  def display_result(self):    #display_result function of derived class
    print("\nTotal Marks:", self.total_marks)
    print("\nPercentage:", self.perc)

r1=result()                          # object of derived class result
r1.display()
r1.display_marks()
r1.display_result()
```

Output

```
Enter Student Name:Richie
Enter RollNo:114
Enter marks of subject 1:43
Enter marks of subject 2:55
Enter marks of subject 3:63


Name:  Richie

RollNo:  114
```

Marks of subject 1= 43.0

Marks of subject 2= 55.0

Marks of subject 3= 63.0

Total Marks: 161.0

Percentage: 53.666666666666664

11.4. Method Overriding in Python

Method overriding is one of the important concepts to consider while using inheritance in Python. As we see in the previous programming Code 11.1. for single inheritance that the __init__() method was defined both in base class as well as derived class. When an object of derived class is created then the __init__() method of derived class overrides that of base class. That means, the __init__() of derived class rectangle takes preference over the __init__() method of shape class.

In order to overcome this issue, the __init__() method of derived class is extended further to make a call to the __init__() method of base class. This is done by using shape.__init__() as shown in the code 11.1. By invoking this way, a call to the __init__() method of shape class is made from the __init__() method of derived class rectangle.

Method overriding can also be resolved by using a built in Python function super(). The super() function invokes the parent constructor method by itself without referring the class name as mentioned in the call shape.__init__(). The super() function is used as follows:

```
super().__init__()
```

The programming illustration of resolving method overriding issue is given in Code 11.4. In this code, the ambiguity in single inheritance is resolved by using the super().__init__() function as highlighted in bold in the code rather than using the shape.__init__(self) method. It is to be noted here that

while calling the constructor method using super() function the __init__()
function does not contain the argument self.

Code: 11.4. Illustration of built-in function super() for single inheritance.

```
#Illustration of resolving method overriding using super()

class shape:                                #base class
    'A shape class'
    def __init__(self):                     #constructor method of base class
        self.length = float(input('Enter Length:'))
        self.breadth = float(input('Enter Breadth:'))


    def display(self):                      #display method of base class
        print ("\nLength: ", self.length)
        print ("\nBreadth: ", self.breadth)


class rectangle(shape):                     #derived class
    'A rectangle class'
    def __init__(self):                     #constructor method of derived class
        super().__init__()
        self.area=0
    def compute_area(self):                 #compute_srea funciton of derived class
        self.area = self.length*self.breadth
        print("\nArea of rectangle=", self.area)


r1=rectangle()              # object of derived class
r1.display()
r1.compute_area()
```
```
Output

Enter Length:12
Enter Breadth:34
Length:  12.0
```

Breadth: 34.0
Area of rectangle= 408.0

In case of multilevel inheritance, the super() function is used as shown in the Code 11.5. In this program, we see that while creating the derived class object r1, the initial call is made to __init__() method of derived class result. Which further invokes the __init__() method of its parent class marks by using the super() function. Furthermore, the __init__() method of marks class invokes its superclass student's __init__() method by using the super() function again. The statement code comprising super() function are highlighted in bold.

Code: 11.5. Illustration of built-in function super() for multilevel inheritance.

```
#Illustration of super(0 function in multilevel inheritance

class student:                          #base class
  'A student class'
  def __init__(self):                   #constructor method of base class
    self.name = (input('Enter Student Name:'))
    self.rollno = int(input('Enter RollNo:'))

  def display(self):                    #display method of
base class
    print ("\nName: ", self.name)
    print ("\nRollNo: ", self.rollno)

class marks(student):                   #derived class
  'A marks class'
  def __init__(self):                   #constructor method of derived class
    super().__init__()
    self.m1 = float(input('Enter marks of subject 1:'))
    self.m2 = float(input('Enter marks of subject 2:'))
    self.m3 = float(input('Enter marks of subject 3:'))
```

```
    def display_marks(self):              #display function of base class 2
        print("\nMarks of subject 1=", self.m1)
        print("\nMarks of subject 2=", self.m2)
        print("\nMarks of subject 3=", self.m3)


class result(marks):                              # new derived class
    'A result class'
    def __init__(self):               #constructor method of new derived class
#    student.__init__(self)
#    marks.__init__(self)
    super().__init__()
    self.total_marks = self.m1 + self.m2 + self.m3
    self.perc = self.total_marks*100/300
    def display_result(self):                  #display_result function of
                                               #derived class

        print("\nTotal Marks:", self.total_marks)
        print("\nPercentage:", self.perc)


r1=result()                               # object of derived class result
r1.display()
r1.display_marks()
r1.display_result()
```

Output

Enter Student Name:Robin
Enter RollNo:222
Enter marks of subject 1:34
Enter marks of subject 2:54
Enter marks of subject 3:55

Name: Robin

RollNo: 222

Marks of subject 1= 34.0

Marks of subject 2= 54.0

Marks of subject 3= 55.0

Total Marks: 143.0

Percentage: 47.666666666666664

In case of multiple inheritance, the super() function is used as presented in Code 11.6. In this code, we see that as there exists two parent classes student and marks. Therefore, while invoking __init__() method using super() function only one of the parent's constructor will be invoked, actually the one which is inherited first by the derived class. For example, the __init__() method of student class will be invoked by using the super() function. In order to make a call to the __init__() method of other parent class marks, we need to use the previous method, which is marks.__init__(self). Therefore, it is to be noted here that in case of multiple inheritance, the super() function invokes the __init__() constructor method of the firstly inherited parent class and to make the call to other parents classes the previous method of using classname with __init__() method is used.

Code: 11.6. Illustration of super() function in multiple inheritance.

```
#Illustration of super() function in multiple inheritance


class student:                    #base class 1
   'A student class'
   def __init__(self):            #constructor method of base class 1
    self.name = (input('Enter Student Name:'))
    self.rollno = int(input('Enter RollNo:'))

   def display(self):             #display method of base class 1
```

```
    print ("\nName: ", self.name)
    print ("\nRollNo: ", self.rollno)


class marks:                          #base class 2
    'A marks class'
    def __init__(self):               #constructor method of base class 2
        self.m1 = float(input('Enter marks of subject 1:'))
        self.m2 = float(input('Enter marks of subject 2:'))
        self.m3 = float(input('Enter marks of subject 3:'))
    def display_marks(self):          #display function of base class 2
        print("\nMarks of subject 1=", self.m1)
        print("\nMarks of subject 2=", self.m2)
        print("\nMarks of subject 3=", self.m3)


class result(student, marks):         #derived class
    'A result class'
    def __init__(self):               #constructor method of derived class
    # student.__init__(self)
        super().__init__()
        marks.__init__(self)
        self.total_marks = self.m1 + self.m2 + self.m3
        self.perc = self.total_marks*100/300
    def display_result(self):         #display_result function of derived class
        print("\nTotal Marks:", self.total_marks)
        print("\nPercentage:", self.perc)


r1=result()                  # object of derived class result
r1.display()
r1.display_marks()
r1.display_result()
```

Output

Enter Student Name: Rachael

```
Enter RollNo:111
Enter marks of subject 1:54
Enter marks of subject 2:65
Enter marks of subject 3:73

Name:  Rachael

RollNo:  111

Marks of subject 1= 54.0

Marks of subject 2= 65.0

Marks of subject 3= 73.0

Total Marks: 192.0

Percentage: 64
```

11.5. Special Functions in Python

The Python language provides two special functions, which can be used while using inheritance. These functions and their description is given in Table 11.1. The programming example for these functions is also given in Code 11.7., the output of which apparently makes clear the use of these functions.

Function	Description
issubclass(child, parent)	Returns a boolean result; either true or false, true if child is indeed a subclass of the superclass parent
isinstance(obj, Class)	Returns a boolean result; either true or false, true if obj is indeed an instance of Class or a subclass of Class

Table 11.1. Python built-in functions for inheritance

Code:11.7. Illustration of ininstance() and issubclass() functions.

```
#Illustration of ininstance() and issubclass() functions

class student:                          #base class
  'A student class'

class marks(student):                   #derived class
  'A marks class'

class result(marks):                    # new derived class
  'A result class'

r1=result()
r2=student()
print(issubclass(result, marks))
print(issubclass(student, marks))
print(isinstance(r1, result))
print(isinstance(r2, result))
```

Output

```
True
False
True
False
```

11.6. Summary

In this chapter, one of the significant features of OOPS known as inheritance is elaborated. Single, multiple, and multilevel inheritance are described with the programming illustration of each. The concept of method overriding is also discussed.

Review Questions

Q.1   What is the significance of inheritance? What are its types?

Q.2   Illustrate single inheritance in Python.

Q.3   Illustrate multiple inheritance in Python.

Q.4   Illustrate multilevel inheritance in Python.

Q.5   What is method overriding? How it is resolved in Python? Explain.

Q.6   List and explain special functions associated with classes in Python.

CHAPTER 12

Python Operator Overloading

Highlights

- Operator overloading
- Overloading arithmetic operators
- Overloading bitwise operators
- Overloading relational operators

In the previous chapter, we learn the fundamentals of OOPS, i.e., the creation of user defined data type classes and objects in Python. In this chapter, we will learn one of the significant features of object oriented programming structures (OOPS) that is operator overloading. As implied from the name, operator overloading means to assign a special meaning to the existing operator to perform some intended task. In other words, same operator exhibiting different meaning as per the situation is called operator overloading. For example, the '+' operator is used to add two numbers, the same can be used for merging two lists and concatenating two strings. It indicates that the same '+' operator can be used to perform different tasks based on the context in which it is being used.

Similarly, two class objects can also be added by using the concept of operator overloading by using the similar syntax that is used for adding two integer numbers. In the following sections, the concept of operator overloading is discussed in detail.

12.1. Overloading '+' Operator in Python

Overloading the '+' operator is quite simpler in Python than C++. The overloaded + operator can add the values contained in two objects by following the same syntax that is used for adding two simple variables. The programming example to overload arithmetic '+' operator is given in Code 12.1. In this program, we see that a class complex is created with two member variables real and imag, which are initialized by using the __init__() constructor function. Then for overloading the plus '+' operator the built-in Python function __add__() is used. This function is specifically meant for adding two objects, which signifies the concept of operator overloading. The user defined function display(), displays the values of object variables.

In this program, we create two objects c1 and c2 of the class complex with initializing values of data members. Then, the values of class data members are displayed associated with these two objects c1 and c2. Subsequently, the addition of two objects c1+c2 is performed by using the same syntax that is used for adding two simple variables. The result of c1+c2 is assigned to a third object c3. Then, the result is displayed by invoking the c3.display() function.

When the statement c1+c2 encounters, it expands as c1.__add__(c2), that means the c1 object invokes the built-in addition overloading function __add__() with c2 as an argument. After the invocation of this function, the control goes to the definition part of __add__() function, where it receives two arguments self and obj. The self object in the argument represents the calling object in the invocation of the function c1.__add__(c2), which is c1 and obj in the argument represents the c2 object, which is passed as an argument. The computation of addition has been performed by accessing the class data members as self.real+obj.real. That means real part of c1 (self) is added with the real part of c2 (obj) and the result is assigned to the real and imag data members of the class. Similar operation is performed for adding the imaginary part. After the computation, both the real and imag variables are returned to the calling function c1+c2, which are received by the c3 object. Subsequently, the result is displayed by calling c3.display(). The output of this code presents the intended result.

Code: 12.1. Illustration of overloading '+' operator in Python

```
#Illustration of arithmetic plus '+' operator overloading

class complex:
        'A complex number class'
        def __init__(self, real, imag):
                self.real=real
                self.imag=imag

        def __add__(self, obj):              #definition of overloading
                                             # '+' operator
                real = self.real + obj.real
                imag = self.imag + obj.imag
                return(complex(real, imag))

        def display(self):
                print(self.real, "+ i",self.imag)

c1=complex(5,6)
c2=complex(7,8)
c1.display()
c2.display()
c3=c1+c2             #overloading '+' operator call
c3.display()
```

Output
5 + i 6
7 + i 8
12 + i 14

12.2. Overloading '-' Operator in Python

Alike, the '+' operator overloading, the subtraction operator '-' can also be overloaded. The programming code for the same is given in Code 12.2. The code is apparently similar to the addition operator overloading for adding up two objects c1 and c2. The only difference is that instead of '+' operator, the '-' operator is used. The built-in Python function used for overloading '-' is __sub__(), which performs the subtraction of two objects and provides the appropriate result. Alike, addition and subtraction operators, other arithmetic operators can also be overloaded. The list of all arithmetic operators with the built-in overloading functions is given in Table 12.1.

Code: 12.2. Illustration of overloading '-' operator in Python

```python
#Illustration of subtraction '-' operator overloading

class complex:
        'A complex number class'
        def __init__(self, real, imag):
                self.real = real
                self.imag = imag

        def __sub__(self, obj):
                real = self.real - obj.real
                imag = self.imag - obj.imag
                return(complex(real, imag))

        def display(self):
                print(self.real, "+ i",self.imag)

c1=complex(5, 8)
```

```
c2=complex(6, 7)
c1.display()
c2.display()
c3=c1-c2
c3.display()
```

Output

5 + i 8
6 + i 7
-1 + i 1

Operator	Expression	Built-in function
Addition (+)	c1 + c2	c1.__add__(c2)
Subtraction (-)	c1 - c2	c1.__sub__(c2)
Multiplication (*)	c1 * c2	c1.__mul__(c2)
Power (**)	c1 ** c2	c1.__pow__(c2)
Division (/)	c1 / c2	c1.__truediv__(c2)
Floor Division (//)	c1 // c2	c1.__floordiv__(c2)
Remainder (modulo) (%)	c1 % c2	c1.__mod__(c2)

Table 12.1. List of Arithmetic Operator Overloading Functions in Python

12.3. Overloading Bitwise Operators

As we know that Python contains a rich set of operators. The bitwise operators can also be overloaded like arithmetic operators. Here in this section, we learn to overload bitwise and operator ('&'). The programming illustration to overload bitwise and (&) operator is given in Code 12.3. As we know that the bitwise and (&) works at bit level and returns true (1) only if both the bits are true (1), otherwise it returns false (0). In this program, we see that a Number class is created, which contains only one data member num. the __init__() method initialize the value of this variable for two objects n1 and n2.

In order to overload the bitwise and (&) operator the invocation is made as n1&n2, where n1 and n2 are the objects of class Number and the result is assigned to the third object n3. The invocation n1&n2 expands as n1.__and__(n2), where __and__() is the built-in Python function for overloading bitwise and operator. In the definition part of this function, n1 represents the calling object that is self and n2 represents the object as argument i.e., obj. The computation is performed by using the dot (.) operator with these two objects self and obj and the bitwise and operator &. The result is returned by typecasting with the class data type Number. The result is received by the object n3 and displayed by calling the n3.display() function. The computation of bitwise and (&) operator over two values 14 and 28 results into 12 as shown in the output.

Code: 12.3. Illustration of overloading bitwise & operator

```
#Illustration of Bitwise '&' operator overloading

class Number:
        'A Number class'
        def __init__(self, num):
                self.num = num

        def __and__(self, obj):
                num = self.num&obj.num
                return(Number(num))

        def display(self):
                print(self.num)

n1=Number(14)
n2=Number(28)
n3=n1&n2
n3.display()
```

Output

12

Similarly, other bitwise operators can be overloaded, the Python built-in functions for them are given in Table 12.2.

Operator	Expression	Built-in function
Bitwise AND	c1 &c2	c1.__and__(c2)
Bitwise OR	c1 | c2	c1.__or__(c2)
Bitwise XOR	c1 ^ c2	c1.__xor__(c2)
Bitwise NOT	~c1	c1.__invert__()
Bitwise Left Shift	c1 << c2	c1.__lshift__(c2)
Bitwise Right Shift	c1 >>c2	c1.__rshift__(c2)
Note: c1 and c2 are objects.		

Table 12.2. List of Bitwise Operator Overloading Functions in Python

12.4. Overloading Relational Operators

The relational operators can also be overloaded as that of arithmetic and bitwise operators. The Python language provides a list of built-in functions for overloading relational operators. As we know that relational operators are less than (<), less than equal to (<=), greater than (>), greater than equal to (>=), equal to (==), and not equal to (!=). Here in this section, we will demonstrate, how to overload greater than (>) relational operator. The programming illustration for the same is given in Code 12.4.

In this program, we create a class distance with two data members a and b. Another built-in function __gt__() is defined in the class with two arguments self and obj. The __gt__() function is used to overload greater than operator in Python. We create two objects d1 and d2 of the class distance. The values of data members have been initialized through constructor __init__() while creating these two objects. Then, the two objects d1 and d2 are compared by using the greater than operator (>), in the same manner in which two simple variables are compared, i.e., d1>d2. Basically, the call d1>d2 expands as d1.__gt__(d2). In the definition part, self in the argument list of __gt__() represents the calling object d1 and obj in the argument list represents d2. Then, the magnitude of the distance is computed for both of the objects and their result is compared and returned as self.mag>obj.mag. As we know that the result of relational expression is either true or false. Therefore, the result for this program is returned as true, which can be seen from the output.

Code: 12.4. Illustration of overloading greater than operator in Python.

```
#Illustration of relational '>' operator overloading

class distance:
        'A distance class'
        def __init__(self, a, b):
                self.a = a
                self.b = b

        def __gt__(self, obj):
                self.mag = self.a**2 + self.b**2
                obj.mag = obj.a**2 + obj.b**2
                return(self.mag>obj.mag)

d1=distance(14, 20)
d2=distance(18, 15)
print(d1>d2)
```

Output

True

Alike, greater than operator other relational operators can also be overloaded. The Python built-in functions for relational operators are given in Table 12.3.

Operator	Expression	Built-in function
Less than	c1 < c2	c1.__lt__(c2)
Less than or equal to	c1 <= c2	c1.__le__(c2)
Equal to	c1 == c2	c1.__eq__(c2)
Not equal to	c1 != c2	c1.__ne__(c2)
Greater than	c1> c2	c1.__gt__(c2)
Greater than or equal to	c1 >= c2	c1.__ge__(c2)
Note: c1 and c2 are objects.		

Table 12.3. List of Relational Operator Overloading Functions in Python

12.5. Summary

In this chapter, we have learned one of the most exciting features of OOPS, which is known as operator overloading. Operator overloading refers to make the same operator to perform different tasks such as the '+' operator which is used to add two numbers can be used to add two objects as well. All the arithmetic operators can be overloaded, where the programming illustration to overload '+' operator is given. Apart from that the bitwise operators and relational operators can also be overloaded. The Python language provides built-in functions for overloading operators. In Python language, to overload an operator is rather simple as that of C++ and Java by using the built-in functions for overloading. The list of all of these functions is given for help supporting the operator overloading.

Review Questions

Q.1   What do you understand by operator overloading? How can you overload an operator in Python?

Q.2   How to overload '+' operator in Python to add two objects?

Q.3   List all the built-in functions for overloading arithmetic operators.

Q.4   How to overload bitwise and (&) operator in Python? Give example.

Q.5   How to overload bitwise or (|) operator in Python? Illustrate.

Q.6   How to overload relational operator greater than (>) in Python? Give example.

Q.7   How to overload relational operator less than (<) in Python?

Q.8   List all the built-in functions to overload bitwise operators in Python.

Q.9   List all the built-in functions to overload relational operators in Python.

Programming Exercises

1)   Write programs to overload following arithmetic operator in Python
      a.   Modulo
      b.   Division

c.   Multiplication
2)   Write programs to overload following bitwise operators in Python
   a.   Bitwise or (|)
   b.   Bitwise and (&)
   c.   Bitwise not (!)
   d.   Bitwise left shift (<<)
   e.   Bitwise right shift (>>)
3)   Write programs to overload following relational operators in Python
   a.   Less than (<)
   b.   Less than equal to (<=)
   c.   Greater than (>)
   d.   Greater than equal to (>=)
   e.   Equal to (==)
   f.   Not equal to (!=)

Appendix-I

List of Python Standard Modules

Module	Description
_	
__future__	Future statement definitions
__main__	The environment where the top-level script is run.
_dummy_thread	Drop-in replacement for the _thread module.
_thread	Low-level threading API.
a	
abc	Abstract base classes according to PEP 3119.
aifc	Read and write audio files in AIFF or AIFC format.
argparse	Command-line option and argument parsing library.
array	Space efficient arrays of uniformly typed numeric values.
ast	Abstract Syntax Tree classes and manipulation.
asynchat	Support for asynchronous command/response protocols.
asyncio	Asynchronous I/O, event loop, coroutines and tasks.
asyncore	A base class for developing asynchronous socket handling services.
atexit	Register and execute cleanup functions.
audioop	Manipulate raw audio data.
b	
base64	RFC 3548: Base16, Base32, Base64 Data Encodings; Base85 and Ascii85
bdb	Debugger framework.

binascii	Tools for converting between binary and various ASCII-encoded binary representations.
binhex	Encode and decode files in binhex4 format.
bisect	Array bisection algorithms for binary searching.
builtins	The module that provides the built-in namespace.
bz2	Interfaces for bzip2 compression and decompression.

c

calendar	Functions for working with calendars, including some emulation of the Unix cal program.
cgi	Helpers for running Python scripts via the Common Gateway Interface.
cgitb	Configurable traceback handler for CGI scripts.
chunk	Module to read IFF chunks.
cmath	Mathematical functions for complex numbers.
cmd	Build line-oriented command interpreters.
code	Facilities to implement read-eval-print loops.
codecs	Encode and decode data and streams.
codeop	Compile (possibly incomplete) Python code.
collections	Container datatypes
colorsys	Conversion functions between RGB and other color systems.
compileall	Tools for byte-compiling all Python source files in a directory tree.
configparser	Configuration file parser.
contextlib	Utilities for with-statement contexts.
copy	Shallow and deep copy operations.
copyreg	Register pickle support functions.
cProfile	
crypt (Unix)	The crypt() function used to check Unix passwords.
csv	Write and read tabular data to and from delimited files.
ctypes	A foreign function library for Python.
curses (Unix)	An interface to the curses library, providing portable terminal handling.

d

datetime	Basic date and time types.
dbm	Interfaces to various Unix "database" formats.
decimal	Implementation of the General Decimal Arithmetic Specification.
difflib	Helpers for computing differences between objects.
dis	Disassembler for Python bytecode.
distutils	Support for building and installing Python modules into an existing Python installation.
doctest	Test pieces of code within docstrings.
dummy_threading	Drop-in replacement for the threading module.

e

email	Package supporting the parsing, manipulating, and generating email messages.
ensurepip	Bootstrapping the "pip" installer into an existing Python installation or virtual environment.
enum	Implementation of an enumeration class.
errno	Standard errno system symbols.

f

faulthandler	Dump the Python traceback.
fcntl (Unix)	The fcntl() and ioctl() system calls.
filecmp	Compare files efficiently.
fileinput	Loop over standard input or a list of files.
fnmatch	Unix shell style filename pattern matching.
formatter	**Deprecated:** Generic output formatter and device interface.
fpectl (Unix)	Provide control for floating point exception handling.
fractions	Rational numbers.
ftplib	FTP protocol client (requires sockets).
functools	Higher-order functions and operations on callable objects.

g

gc	Interface to the cycle-detecting garbage collector.
getopt	Portable parser for command line options; support both short and long option names.
getpass	Portable reading of passwords and retrieval of the userid.
gettext	Multilingual internationalization services.
glob	Unix shell style pathname pattern expansion.
grp (Unix)	The group database (getgrnam() and friends).
gzip	Interfaces for gzip compression and decompression using file objects.

h

hashlib	Secure hash and message digest algorithms.
heapq	Heap queue algorithm (a.k.a. priority queue).
hmac	Keyed-Hashing for Message Authentication (HMAC) implementation
html	Helpers for manipulating HTML.
http	HTTP status codes and messages

i

imaplib	IMAP4 protocol client (requires sockets).
imghdr	Determine the type of image contained in a file or byte stream.
imp	**Deprecated:** Access the implementation of the import statement.
importlib	The implementation of the import machinery.
inspect	Extract information and source code from live objects.
io	Core tools for working with streams.
ipaddress	IPv4/IPv6 manipulation library.
itertools	Functions creating iterators for efficient looping.

j

json	Encode and decode the JSON format.

k

keyword	Test whether a string is a keyword in Python.

l

lib2to3	the 2to3 library
linecache	This module provides random access to individual lines from text files.
locale	Internationalization services.
logging	Flexible event logging system for applications.
lzma	A Python wrapper for the liblzma compression library.

m

macpath	Mac OS 9 path manipulation functions.
mailbox	Manipulate mailboxes in various formats
mailcap	Mailcap file handling.
marshal	Convert Python objects to streams of bytes and back (with different constraints).
math	Mathematical functions (sin() etc.).
mimetypes	Mapping of filename extensions to MIME types.
mmap	Interface to memory-mapped files for Unix and Windows.
modulefinder	Find modules used by a script.
msilib (Windows)	Creation of Microsoft Installer files, and CAB files.
msvcrt (Windows)	Miscellaneous useful routines from the MS VC++ runtime.
multiprocessing	Process-based parallelism.

n

netrc	Loading of .netrc files.
nis (Unix)	Interface to Sun's NIS (Yellow Pages) library.
nntplib	NNTP protocol client (requires sockets).

numbers	Numeric abstract base classes (Complex, Real, Integral, etc.).

o

operator	Functions corresponding to the standard operators.
optparse	**Deprecated:** Command-line option parsing library.
os	Miscellaneous operating system interfaces.
ossaudiodev (Linux, FreeBSD)	Access to OSS-compatible audio devices.

p

parser	Access parse trees for Python source code.
pathlib	Object-oriented filesystem paths
pdb	The Python debugger for interactive interpreters.
pickle	Convert Python objects to streams of bytes and back.
pickletools	Contains extensive comments about the pickle protocols and pickle-machine opcodes, as well as some useful functions.
pipes (Unix)	A Python interface to Unix shell pipelines.
pkgutil	Utilities for the import system.
platform	Retrieves as much platform identifying data as possible.
plistlib	Generate and parse Mac OS X plist files.
poplib	POP3 protocol client (requires sockets).
posix (Unix)	The most common POSIX system calls (normally used via module os).
pprint	Data pretty printer.
profile	Python source profiler.
pstats	Statistics object for use with the profiler.
pty (Linux)	Pseudo-Terminal Handling for Linux.
pwd (Unix)	The password database (getpwnam() and friends).
py_compile	Generate byte-code files from Python source files.
pyclbr	Supports information extraction for a Python class browser.

| pydoc | Documentation generator and online help system. |

q

| queue | A synchronized queue class. |
| quopri | Encode and decode files using the MIME quoted-printable encoding. |

r

random	Generate pseudo-random numbers with various common distributions.
re	Regular expression operations.
readline (Unix)	GNU readline support for Python.
reprlib	Alternate repr() implementation with size limits.
resource (Unix)	An interface to provide resource usage information on the current process.
rlcompleter	Python identifier completion, suitable for the GNU readline library.
runpy	Locate and run Python modules without importing them first.

s

sched	General purpose event scheduler.
secrets	Generate secure random numbers for managing secrets.
select	Wait for I/O completion on multiple streams.
selectors	High-level I/O multiplexing.
shelve	Python object persistence.
shlex	Simple lexical analysis for Unix shell-like languages.
shuti	High-level file operations, including copying.
signal	Set handlers for asynchronous events.
site	Module responsible for site-specific configuration.
smtpd	A SMTP server implementation in Python.
smtplib	SMTP protocol client (requires sockets).
sndhdr	Determine type of a sound file.

socket	Low-level networking interface.
socketserver	A framework for network servers.
spwd (Unix)	The shadow password database (getspnam() and friends).
sqlite3	A DB-API 2.0 implementation using SQLite 3.x.
ssl	TLS/SSL wrapper for socket objects
stat	Utilities for interpreting the results of os.stat(), os.lstat() and os.fstat().
statistics	mathematical statistics functions
string	Common string operations.
stringprep	String preparation, as per RFC 3453
struct	Interpret bytes as packed binary data.
subprocess	Subprocess management.
sunau	Provide an interface to the Sun AU sound format.
symbol	Constants representing internal nodes of the parse tree.
symtable	Interface to the compiler's internal symbol tables.
sys	Access system-specific parameters and functions.
sysconfig	Python's configuration information
syslog (Unix)	An interface to the Unix syslog library routines.

t

tabnanny	Tool for detecting white space related problems in Python source files in a directory tree.
tarfile	Read and write tar-format archive files.
telnetlib	Telnet client class.
tempfile	Generate temporary files and directories.
termios (Unix)	POSIX style tty control.
test	Regression tests package containing the testing suite for Python.
textwrap	Text wrapping and filling
threading	Thread-based parallelism.
time	Time access and conversions.
timeit	Measure the execution time of small code snippets.
tkinter	Interface to Tcl/Tk for graphical user interfaces
token	Constants representing terminal nodes of the parse tree.

tokenize	Lexical scanner for Python source code.
trace	Trace or track Python statement execution.
traceback	Print or retrieve a stack traceback.
tracemalloc	Trace memory allocations.
tty (Unix)	Utility functions that perform common terminal control operations.
turtle	An educational framework for simple graphics applications
turtledemo	A viewer for example turtle scripts
types	Names for built-in types.
typing	Support for type hints (see PEP 484).

u

unicodedata	Access the Unicode Database.
unittest	Unit testing framework for Python.
urllib	
uu	Encode and decode files in uuencode format.
uuid	UUID objects (universally unique identifiers) according to RFC 4122

v

venv	Creation of virtual environments.

w

warnings	Issue warning messages and control their disposition.
wave	Provide an interface to the WAV sound format.
weakref	Support for weak references and weak dictionaries.
webbrowser	Easy-to-use controller for Web browsers.
winreg (Windows)	Routines and objects for manipulating the Windows registry.
winsound (Windows)	Access to the sound-playing machinery for Windows.
wsgire	WSGI Utilities and Reference Implementation.

X

xdrlib	Encoders and decoders for the External Data Representation (XDR).
xml	Package containing XML processing modules

Z

zipapp	Manage executable python zip archives
zipfile	Read and write ZIP-format archive files.
zipimport	support for importing Python modules from ZIP archives.
zlib	Low-level interface to compression and decompression routines compatible with gzip.

Bibliography

M. C. Brown, The Complete Reference Python, Osborne/McGraw-Hill, 2001.

S. Maruch, A. Maruch, Python for Dummies, John Wiley & Sons, 2011.

A. B. Downey, Think Python, O'Reilly Media Inc., 2012.

B. Slatkin, Effective Python, Addison Wesley Professional, 2015.

J. M. Zelle, Python Programming: An Introduction to Computer Science, Franklin, Beedle & Associates, Inc., 2004.

A. Downey, J. Elkner, C. Meyers, How to Think Like a Computer Scientist Learning with Python, Green Tea Press, Wellesley, Massachusetts, 2002.

M. Lutz, Python Pocket Reference, O'Reilly Media, 2014

A.Martelli, Python in a Nutshell: A Desktop Quick Reference, O'Reilly Media, 2006

Index

Made in the USA
Coppell, TX
25 September 2022

83601040R00173